Creating a Culture of Valued Leadership

Engaging and Retaining Talented People
for Your organization

Michael G. Gerken

Mission Point Press

Readers are encouraged to go to www.MissionPointPress.com to contact the author or to find information on how to buy this book in bulk at a discounted rate.

Published by Mission Point Press
2554 Chandler Lake Rd.
Traverse City, MI 49686
(231) 421-9513

www.MissionPointPress.com

Cover photography by Don Ipock.

ISBN: 978-1-943995-05-9

Library of Congress Control Number: 2016938345

Printed in the United States of America.

Life is far too short to allow our valuable professional and volunteer time to be spent in organizational environments where we do not "get to play." The better organizations are at creating **cultures of valued leadership,** *the more they benefit from the leadership contributions of their associates.*

This book is dedicated to the people who
have shared lessons learned from their life
experiences and helped me value the process
of being a student of my life experiences.

To all of you, I say thanks.

Carl, thanks for all the valued leadership you have delivered to so many significant organizations and projects. You are an inspiration to everyone in Kansas City.

Mike Gerber

Acknowledgements

Some material shared in this book was developed in the context of my 45-year career with Waddell & Reed, a national financial services organization headquartered in Kansas City. I am grateful to the many people there who let me create and try out my organizational development ideas. They helped me become a better professional and a better person.

Special thanks go to all the people I reported to and people who, theoretically, reported to me. Lessons came from all of them. I learned to listen and collaborate. I learned that people are interested and interesting. I learned that, if you are genuinely inquisitive (not nosy), people enjoy sharing their insights. I learned that good questions lead to new insights.

Over time I was presented with opportunities to teach and coach which really meant that I was teaching and coaching myself. So, thanks to everyone who shared and gave me those opportunities.

Here are a few people who deserve a special thank-you:

To my first bosses, **Ross Williams and Carl Shortino,** thank you for welcoming me into the business world. Your patience and respect had a powerful influence on me and my career.

To **Rebecca,** who left our world far too soon, thanks for encouraging me to **be real** and to **be present** in the moments of my life.

To my wife, **Debra,** thank you for sharing your life with me and for your continuing encouragement and patience as I wrote this book. And thanks for editing my words with finesse and kindness.

To my children, **Eric, Gina and Jason,** thanks for all the lessons you have taught me about life. Thanks for tolerating my rambling conversations about book ideas and for your willingness to ask some great questions.

Thanks to my **grandchildren** who kept asking me, "Aren't you done with your book yet?"

Thanks to my former MBA professor, **Bill Eddy,** who listened, challenged me with questions, and offered very insightful suggestions for the book. Of course, you would expect that from a former dean of the University of Missouri–Kansas City School of Business.

Thanks to my friends **Donn Wadley,** a wise educator and proud California Rotarian, and **Charlie Collins**, a wise jazz educator, musician and patient fly fishing instructor. Both have encouraged me to continue writing, offered valuable critiques, and been great jazz festival companions.

Contents

Author's Preface

This book is about you and the organizations where you contribute your time and talent. It explores a simple, impactful leadership concept along with specific tactics you can use to enable your organizations to be more interesting, innovative, and effective.

Most books, articles and programs on leadership focus on skills, perspectives, and practices of being **the** leader. This book focuses on helping **you** influence your organizations, whether they are for-profit or not-for-profit, small or large, to become cultures where all associates are encouraged to contribute leadership.

Increasingly we see organizations struggle to attract, engage and retain people. We see repeated examples of breakdowns in the ability of public and private organizations to deliver valued services. Their associates lose enthusiasm, lessen their level of engagement, and move on. The organizations then struggle to develop the knowledge, skills and institutional insights which are needed to create broader competency and deliver value. They miss opportunities. The consumers of their products and services lose confidence and search for alternatives. Their investors look for a better story.

I believe that organizations where all associates/employees are encouraged to contribute leadership are able to attract, engage, and retain talented people. They create a stronger story that associates enjoy sharing with their peers, vital stakeholders, and new associates. They identify and capture new opportunities. They become pillars of their industries and their communities.

I wrote this book for two reasons. First, several people who should have known better challenged me to write down the observations and practices I had subjected my associates to for many years. Second, I wanted to share what I have learned from my experiences.

As I wrote, I pondered whether my perspectives are really just about how I want organizations to operate, or whether those perspectives and related tactics are valid for others to utilize. My conclusion is that they are both valid and advantageous.

I do recognize that my perspectives may be a challenge for organizations dominated by leaders who are overly enamored with their own authority. For those so disposed, I offer this observation: The perspectives I share are not from a context of "shared leadership" or diminishing someone's authority; they are from a context of increasing the value of the people key to that leader's personal success.

During my forty-five-year career in the financial services industry, I held multiple leadership titles and sets of responsibilities. I served in leadership roles with a variety of civic, not-for-profit, and professional organizations. I participated in many leadership-focused seminars, and conducted hundreds of meetings and conferences for people in leadership roles.

I have studied hundreds of books on management and leadership. I have read biographies and historical accounts of people who, through praise or blame, became famous for what did or did not happen during their time in front of the masses.

I have read countless leadership-focused articles with titles like: "The Five Principles," "The Six Keys," "The Critical Do's and Don'ts," "The New Do's and Don'ts," "The Magic Practices," and "The Secrets to Leadership in Today's Environment." Although my study and experience convince me that the opportunities and complexities of leadership do not fit into such neat packages, I find interesting the perspectives of people engaged in influencing themselves, their peers, their practices, and their outcomes.

I have learned this:

Organizations that create what I identify as **_cultures of valued leadership_** versus cultures where just **the** leaders are valued:

- Become places where people are proud to share a piece of their lives.
- Deserve and receive their associates' best efforts.
- Attract and retain more than their share of great talent.
- Expand their capacity to innovate and improve outcomes.
- Are places where people enjoy contributing their talent.

I have also learned that creating and participating in such cultures **benefits you.**

Life is far too short to allow our professional and volunteer time to be spent in organizations where we do not "get to play," i.e., contribute leadership through our role in the organization.

The chapters of this book explore how you can create environments of leadership. The ideas shared can generate new leadership for your organizations. They can enable you to deliver valued leadership.

Introduction

For a significant portion of my career, I had the words *"professional development"* in my title. I had the opportunity to teach people to be leaders of their professional lives. I am proud of that. I love the idea that our personal and professional development is about recognizing that **we are the leaders of our lives**. That idea reinforces the opportunities, challenges, and fun of being a student of our life experiences. It enables us to grasp that proactiveness beats reactiveness. It enables us to grasp that the ***world of opportunities is a great place to live.***

I believe each of us creates opportunities to positively advance by first finding ways to **listen** and **learn**. Then we continue to positively progress by finding ways to **teach** and **coach**. I think organizations create opportunities to progress by doing those same things, in that order.

Organizations also create and capture opportunities to advance when they engage multiple points of leadership.

As you read this book, view the ideas presented in the context of your personal interactions within the organizations where you have contributed, or currently are contributing, your time. Your personal experiences will be your learning lab.

The first three chapters lay the foundation for the ideas shared in the rest of the book. After reading them, you can jump around as you see fit. Every chapter will give you specific ideas you can customize for yourself and apply in your sphere of influence.

I found the process of compiling this material to be a great learning experience. My hope is that you will find the material beneficial as you explore your world of leadership opportunities.

Creating a Culture of Valued Leadership

Chapter 1

It's Your Time and Talent- Where Will You Spend It?

We were born. We learned to eat, move around, and talk.
Things were good. Food showed up. We got to take naps. We
became aware that people other than our primary caretakers
existed. Then, without even grasping the concept, we became
participants in an organization. Oh sure this group did not
have an organization chart or mission statement, but we were
in it. It started small with just a few pals interacting with
resources that the big people called toys. And since we were
observant little creatures, we quickly noticed that other little
creatures in the organization were trying to influence stuff.
They were trying to influence style, practices, and outcomes.
And so were we. Thus began our life's involvement with
organizations.

The idea that an organization succeeds because of **the** leader is a
fallacy.

Organizations are fascinating creatures. They are assembled, analyzed,
diagnosed, dissected, and reassembled. They are critiqued, maligned,
and occasionally complimented. They are subjected to a myriad of
management approaches. They continuously seek leadership.

For fifty-plus years I have observed myself and others attempt to influence style, practices, and outcomes of groups that had organization charts and mission statements. My professional focus for many of those years was helping organizations expand their capacity to pursue their purpose for existence. The catalyst to expanding that capacity was the continuing professional development of their people's knowledge and skills. A key component of that professional development was leadership.

My years of observations, combined with a growing desire to leave a meaningful legacy, led me to concentrate on creating a unique, sustainable development model for people in leadership roles in my organization. The foundation of the model was selection based on a concept of readiness. The desired outcomes for the model included every leader being respected for their preparation, effectiveness, and continuous professional development. Another desired outcome was for the team of leaders to become a recognized and respected leadership brand within their industry.

While working on this model I pondered many questions. Here are a few of them:

Q – What can be an effective model to attract, select, develop, and retain leaders?

Q – Why is our current model not generating all of our desired outcomes?

Q – What was, or could be, our organization's uniqueness in the industry?

Q – How could the advantages of that uniqueness be captured?

Q – What were our underlying professional beliefs? Were they valid?

Q – How would the concept of readiness be integrated into the model?

Q – How wide and deep should be the curriculum to build knowledge and skills?

Q – How could I describe the vision, the mission for the program?

Q – What better questions could I be asking?

While obsessing over these questions, I was also searching for a phrase to describe the vision for these efforts. I had written multiple rambling paragraphs seeking to describe what I was pursuing.

Then, one day I wrote the following phrase: ***Culture of_____ leadership.***

I positioned this phrase on my desk so I could not avoid seeing it. Each day, as I worked to create new leadership development models, I pondered what word or words to insert in the blank space. After a few weeks, I put the paper with the written phrase in my billfold next to my lucky $2 bill. The phrase traveled with me everywhere. I took it out frequently, stared at it, and pondered. I was concerned that I would start talking to the paper like Tom Hanks talked to his volleyball in the movie *Cast Away*.

As I searched for answers to my list of questions and for the word to fit the blank space, my efforts to create new development programs were being impacted by some professional observations that I viewed as "realities." Here they are:

Reality # 1- Preference for Commonality.

Organizations prefer more commonality of business practices, not less. By commonality I mean everyone in the organization utilizes the same models, practices, procedures, and programs. My organization's collective bias (group think), as is the bias of most organizations, was that the more commonality of training and execution, the better the efficiency and, hopefully, the better the effectiveness. Nice, sensible theory. But ponder this—I never wanted to be a clone of someone else. Did you?

More commonality can reduce the breadth of subjects to teach and coach. It can reduce the inconsistencies of how activities are executed. It does not, however, address another reality.

Reality #2- Yes, We Are Different.

People are different. They take pride in that reality. And the differences they bring to the organization become the heart and soul as well as the source of potential for the organization.

While planning and facilitating meetings, conferences, and workshops for people with leadership titles, I observed thousands of interactions. I watched and listened as the participants shared how they did what they did. They agreed, disagreed, challenged, debated, and tried to sell each other on the validity of their approaches. They laid evident their styles, biases, professional beliefs, dominant tendencies, and self-imposed limitations. Some were proud of skills they did not yet possess. Some were not sufficiently proud of skills they did possess.

Their differences were amazing, and yet they were all people involved in the processes of influencing outcomes. Given the reality of this diversity, what were the implications concerning design and delivery of programs that could assist people to improve their performance and results? And what was the word that would fit the blank space on the slip of paper next to my lucky $2 bill?

Reality #3- We Are Where We Are.

People are always at different places on their paths to acquire knowledge and skills. They have different levels of competency and professionalism. They may be significantly down the path of product knowledge but have barely stepped on the path of conversational skills to uncover clients' needs and wants. Given this reality, what were the implications on design and delivery of resources and programs?

Reality #4- Leadership Doesn't Fit One Model.

People can only lead effectively when they do so in a manner consistent with their uniqueness. There is no one model or one personality of effective leadership. People cannot lead by trying to be someone else. Individuality is inherent to the realness required to be an effective leader.

Reality #5- Leadership Is Not a Simple Thing to Describe, Teach or Learn.

Generally, leadership is about influencing: influencing the vision for the organization's future, the performance results of the people involved, the ways markets are engaged, and yes, influencing ourselves as well as those we consider to be our leaders. But, exactly how is that taught or learned?

Given my many questions and these realities, what could be the ingredients of an effective, professional development model? And what was the word that could fit on my piece of paper that acknowledged these realities?

One morning I heard myself ask this question: *Regardless of their different styles, what could be said about leaders I had observed who were valued for their positive impacts on both people and outcomes?* And there it was: the word I wanted. The word was **"valued."** If those leaders influenced others to achieve positive outcomes, regardless of their level of knowledge, skill, style, or professional beliefs, **their leadership was valued!**

This concept acknowledges that regardless of the **infinity of differences of leaders**, if they positively influence people and outcomes, they are valued. The **valued leadership** concept:

Recognizes **uniqueness.**

Fosters **realness** of individual spirit and style.

Promotes **progress, inventiveness,** and **entrepreneurial thinking.**

Valued leadership begins with our personal mindset. Ask yourself:

Q – Do you value what you do and how you do it? Do others?

Q – If not, what new practices and roles are a better match for your interests?

Q – What incremental knowledge and skill would increase your leadership value?

Q – Who could become your mentor to help you enhance your value?

I love this idea of valued leadership. Being valued becomes the **mission for leaders**. It also becomes a **teaching, coaching, and mentoring** message that encourages leadership thinking.

Now, let me share how this valued leadership concept evolved into a broader and, I believe, significantly more impactful concept for organizations.

Chapter 2

Cultures of Valued Leadership-
The More Powerful Story

Every organization has its own culture, planned or not, of assumptions, beliefs, attitudes, guidelines, practices, biases, and, of course, some dysfunctional behavior. This is true even if the organization is comprised only of an entrepreneur and a few support vendors.

An organization's culture can be influenced by well-worded mission and vision statements. It can be bolstered by occasional "rally the troops" slogans. Its weaknesses can be obscured, in the short term, by flashy talking points and "We believe" speeches. But the real culture is reflective of the collective behaviors of all the people in the organization. Since I was focused on the development of people who carried around organizational titles that implied they were in a leadership role, I had been focused on creating a phrase to describe only that component of the organization's culture.

As I repeated to myself and others the definition of the organization's culture being the "collective behaviors of all of us," even though I was really just referring to people with leadership titles, I began to grasp the potential for a broader concept of valued leadership for organizations.

The concept is that **every participant** can contribute leadership to an organization, regardless of whether it is large or small, for-profit or not-for-profit. That perspective, that story, is more valuable and powerful. It becomes a **multiplier of energy, creativity, opportunities, and solutions.**

Let's be clear. This concept does not mean that everyone gets to be "in charge," make decisions for, or obstruct decisions made by the organization. Let's not get crazy. It merely refers to the reality that every participant has the capacity **to observe and listen so they can learn and contribute.**

Regardless of title or assignments, each associate can deliver leadership through their individual roles. Each person can share perspectives, deliver fresh thought, ask better questions, and seek more understanding. Each person can positively influence progress. As their knowledge, skills and understanding increase, their ability to deliver valued leadership expands.

By creating an environment of practices that promote leadership thinking and action from all associates, the organization becomes a culture of valued leadership.

I am on a campaign to *create cultures of valued leadership* versus cultures where only **"the"** leader or leaders are valued, and certainly versus cultures where the motto seems to be, "this is the way we do it and you will like it." Your time, talents, purpose, and passions are too valuable to stay in such environments.

I want to help you help your organizations become *cultures of valued leadership*. These cultures are healthy and dynamic. They define the mission for all associates. That mission is to be valued.

Note: While in my professional capacity with the financial services firm, Waddell & Reed, Inc., I initiated the use of the phrase, "Creating a culture of valued leadership." That phrase was used to describe and promote the organization's leadership development programs.

Chapter 3

What Does a Culture of Valued Leadership Look Like?

So let's say you are interested in creating a community where leadership of thought and action is encouraged, acknowledged, and reinforced. What actions can you take to move in that direction?

Before we examine actions to take, let's consider how we might describe an organization where a culture of valued leadership exists.

Assume an organization with these components:

> ▶ *People engaged in* **distribution** *of products and/or services. (Who doesn't have this?)*

- In the financial services industry, these people are usually referred to as advisors.
- In other industries they might be called sales specialists, consultants, or rainmakers.

> ▶ *People who serve as* **leaders/managers** *of those people. (Who doesn't have this?)*

▶ *Multiple functional* "silos." *(Who doesn't have this?)*

- By "silos," I mean departments, areas of special knowledge or, depending on my mood, I may mean "where the crazy, irrational, nothing-matters-but-them" people live.
- In larger organizations, these silos include marketing, sales, accounting, and finance.
- Silos can consist of one person or many people.
- In smaller entrepreneur environments, the silos may take the form of biases of past experiences, assumptions, and vendor advice (valid or not).

Given this scenario, how could we know a culture of valued leadership exists? It exists when:

▶ **Sales specialists** recognize *and* value *the* leadership they bring *to:*

- **Creating, enhancing, and retaining** client relationships.
- **Enhancing** their **personal business** model.
- **Advancing** their **personal professional skills and knowledge.**

▶ *Clients recognize the benefits of the* leadership *and* advocacy *of their advisor, specialist, consultant.*

▶ *Designated leaders are* respected *for their:*

- **Preparation** and **effectiveness.**
- **Capacity** to create and enhance associate relationships.
- **Efforts to enhance the capabilities and capacity** of their teams.
- Continuous **personal professional development.**

▶ *All associates* recognize and value *their opportunities to bring leadership to their roles.*

Note that these descriptions are not about increased sales or profit margins. They are about attitudes, perspectives, professional beliefs, and resulting practices. This package of ingredients reflects a culture where leadership of thought and action is encouraged, acknowledged, and reinforced. That culture becomes the catalyst to enhanced success metrics such as increased sales and profit margins.

This culture's foundation is **acknowledgement** that the opportunity to deliver leadership thought exists. In this scenario, for example, once an advisor **truly recognizes** that she or he is **the leader** of **creating, enhancing, and retaining** client relationships they can:

- Create unique value for their target markets.
- Specialize in challenges they and their clients find most interesting.
- Identify and pursue expanded knowledge and skills.
- Deliver value that clients did not even know was available.

In short, they **become valued** for their **leadership**. They are not just a "commodity" in the marketplace.

In addition to your professional situation, if you are involved in civic groups or other not-for-profits, when would you know that a culture of valued leadership exists in those organizations?

Apply This Concept to Your Organizations

Using the situation described above as your model, complete the following blanks for one of the organizations where you are employed or contribute your valuable time.

My organization would have a **culture where leadership of thought and action** is encouraged, acknowledged, and reinforced when:

Officers/Designated Leaders are respected for:

- _____

- _____

Associates/Members recognize and value:

- _____

- _____

Specialists/Support People/Vendors recognize and value:

- _____

- _____

Clients/Participants recognize/benefit from:

- _____

- _____

Let's now examine some ingredients and steps you can use to move your organizations to be places where leadership thought and action is encouraged, acknowledged, and reinforced.

Take comfort.

None of what will be shared requires dramatic speeches, major kick-off meetings, or expensive retreats. You will not have to confess to everyone that you have, once again, read a book on management or leadership. And you will not need to ask everyone to change their personalities or compensation models.

We start by examining the language of leadership.

Chapter 4

"Get-To" Beats "Got-To"

Leadership language is relatively simple. From my perspective it boils down to this idea: **"Get-to"** beats **"got-to," "need-to," "have-to," "should,"** and **"must."** It also beats the ever popular **"Until we do X, we can't do...can't initiate...can't accomplish Y."**

An organization's culture is reflective of its dialogue, both spoken and written. This is particularly true concerning leadership-oriented language, i.e., language aimed at shaping mindsets and influencing people, practices, and outcomes.

Occasionally the language of leadership takes the form of major announcements or well- crafted speeches. Sometimes it happens during impassioned interactions in conference rooms or behind closed office doors. Most of the time, however, the reality of leadership culture is influenced and reflected by everyday conversations.

It is easy to spot "get-to" versus "got-to" oriented language. The next time you listen to commentary-oriented podcasts, TV, radio (or other forms of communication that people my age do not even know exist), notice how frequently you hear **"We've got to ...We must...We need to...We have to..."** phrases. This will be true whether the shows are focused on sports, politics, or fitness. Do these phrases lead people to expanded thinking and new possibilities? Or do they lead people to need new shoe leather because they dig their heels in to defend their turf of ideas?

The next time you are in an organizational setting, observe the frequency of "got-to" versus "get-to" conversations. "Got-to" oriented conversations can easily arise from a *"That is what we have always done and how we have always done it"* perspective. That perspective may generate new ideas about how things can be done more efficiently. That can be a good result. However, when we add a "get-to" perspective into the conversations, a broader range of possibilities will be identified. That is a better result.

When wrapped in "We have to" or "We need to" phrases, what is being discussed becomes a burden rather than an opportunity. These parental sounding phrases narrow the collective mindset, diminish the group's capacity to seek broader thinking, and discourage participants from participating.

This is easy to see if you have children or grandchildren. Watch their look of utter giddiness when you tell them, **"They must/they have to** (insert your favorite example)." Ok, so giddiness is not the reaction you see. Now put yourself on the receiving end of a **"You have to** (insert your favorite example)." Look in the mirror and take your pulse. See or feel any giddiness?

Orienting our language into positive phrasing creates significant changes in receptivity and attitudes. "Get-to" phrases encourage. "Get-to" phrases create mindsets open to opportunities.

It is not unusual for a symptom of a problem to be viewed as the thing to be fixed. Without encouraging broader thinking, the symptom may get addressed but the bigger opportunities will be missed. When "got-to" oriented language dominates conversations, participants' mindsets narrow. Fixing, rather than innovating, becomes the norm.

In a problem-focused environment, it will be no challenge for people to be busy. It will, however, be a challenge for people to be effective.

Scenario- Moving "We've got to" into "We get to."

Let's say market research indicates that your organization **must** increase/reduce/modify its primary product. You are in a conference room, actual or virtual, that is full of people who have worked hard to create this product's features, marketing resources, sales tactics, profit-margin analysis, and tracking metrics. Now you get to deliver the findings of the market research. The data gathered indicates that the product, although initially successful, is now gasping for market share oxygen.

You have a perfect **"We've got to"** scenario.

So after you or the high priced consultants present the data, do you then say some version of, *"Obviously, **we've got to** make changes and we must do it now" or "How did we misjudge and execute this so badly?"*

Assuming you did not fall off the novice leadership truck yesterday, and you have read more than your share of Dilbert comics, you will likely have a more enlightened approach. Your leadership finesse will kick in, you will solicit questions and reactions, and perhaps even offer opportunities for spear-chucking aimed at the consultants or the data. But after this initial interaction and fun, the conversation can still easily denigrate into a "we've got to" summary that obstructs opportunity-focused thinking and participation.

This will likely be followed with the organizational equivalent of "Don't tell Dad but…" conversations. Participants will be saying to each other statements like: *"Why didn't they just save time and tell us we **have to** do what they've already decided we have to do… They don't want to hear our thoughts or suggestions… They don't care that we know more than they do… How are we expected to fit this into our other deadlines?"*

So let's move this process from a **"got-to"** to a **"get-to"** mindset that reinforces a culture where leadership of thought from all participants is encouraged.

Again, assume the data is presented to the group either by you or by the irritating, know-it-all but responsible-for-nothing consultants. (I just threw that in to relieve some past, not-yet-released resentment that

I was not able to resolve through normal levels of passive-aggressive behavior.) Then you share a version of the following:

*"Everyone here has great knowledge of the features and benefits of this product. We worked hard to get it ready. We know how we positioned it for our markets. Now we have fresh data that creates opportunities for us to gain insight and bring fresh thought to our assumptions, approaches, and potential next steps. We **get-to** _____."*

Following this opening, you can move immediately to relevant, open-ended questions that demonstrate that leadership of thought from everyone is valued. Potential questions include:

Q– *What surprised you about the data?*

Q– *What additional clarifying data would be useful?*

Q– *How can we leverage what we learned about buyers' decisions/ satisfaction?*

Q– *What opportunities do you see?*

- *Re-branding?*
- *Increase/decrease/modify the features?*
- *Concentrate resources in specific market segments?*
- *Increase training?*

The foundation of this process is trust. Trust evolves from consistency of experience. If participants have been conditioned by repeated "got-to" proclamation approaches, their mindset will be on quick fixes and avoiding yet another "got-to" being added to their to-do list. Their initial reaction to the above trust-based process may be one of these:

- *"We are being played and this will not turn out well for us."*
- *"Holy cow—our leader has read a leadership article that included the idea of treating us as adults."*

Either way, here are two approaches you can use prior to asking questions:

Approach 1 - Fess up that you:

- Regret not having created an environment where the talent and ingenuity of all associates is encouraged to be shared.
- Assume everyone wants to contribute.
- Welcome questions and perspective sharing.
- Recognize that people have not felt comfortable posing questions and challenging assumptions.
- Want to focus on opportunities.
- Want to create a culture where everyone shares leadership of thought and action.

Approach 2 - Just jump in and pose questions like those above.

Whichever approach is used, once dialogue begins, **listen, acknowledge, clarify, and reinforce** positive interactions. Make sure everyone speaks. Take notes. The result is that both you and the other participants can gain understanding.

You will find it interesting how collaborative initiatives will spontaneously appear and new opportunities will be identified. Because people participated in this trust-based approach, they will be willing and prepared to move to specific next steps. A culture that values leadership of thought and action will be reinforced.

Scenario - Not-for-Profit Organization

Assume you chair the board of a not-for-profit organization. The Board Executive Committee and senior staff members have been provided information that indicates the organization **must** increase/reduce/modify (pick your favorite item based on your past experiences).

The board members, all volunteers, have varying levels of knowledge about the organization's mission, vision, practices, resources, and financials. They have accountability for governance and results but do not directly manage staff or operations. Each of them have committed financially to the organization. And each of them has demonstrated their capacity to express strong opinions.

Now assume you are leading a meeting with senior staff and the board of directors. The new, not positive information is presented. It indicates that although the organization's services have historically been well perceived and utilized, these services are now gasping for "relevance" oxygen.

Again, we have a perfect **"We-must"** scenario.

After the data is shared, the fun of teeth gnashing and finger pointing begins. (This is sometimes referred to in management literature as organizational dynamics.) In your role as board chair you own the responsibility of opening the conversation. Do you initiate this process by sharing some version of, *"Obviously, we **must** make changes and we **must** do it now,"* or *"How did we deliver our services so poorly that their value is being questioned and our mission is being diminished?"*

Let's assume that your better angels show up, you skip the **"we-must"** (or even worse **"you-must"**) opening to discussions, and you start with your version of the following:

*"Everyone here has demonstrated their belief and commitment to our mission. We value the services we make possible. We all work diligently to see that our services make a positive difference and are delivered efficiently and effectively. We know our clients benefit from our services. Now we have fresh information that indicates gaps in our perspectives versus those of our clients. We can utilize this information to evaluate our assumptions and practices. **We get to** (identify appropriate next steps, etc.)."*

With that foundation, you can move to relevant, open-ended questions inviting everyone to participate. As in the previous example, you may want to first offer an opportunity for venting and questioning the validity of the information. Everyone enjoys attacking the messenger of negative news. Then you can move to questions that reinforce your trust-based approach that values leadership thinking by everyone. Questions might include:

Q– *Reflect on the last few conversations you have had with our clients. Do you think their feedback was reflective of the new data we have been given?*

Q– *What additional question could we have asked them?*

Q– *How can the client experience be enhanced based on what we learned about:*

- The factors that lead them to utilize our services initially?

- Level of understanding/expectations/satisfaction with services used?

Q– *What feedback have we received recently from potential clients who chose not to utilize our services?*

Q– *What factors have led people to discontinue using our services?*

Q– *What feedback have we received recently from our patrons who are enabling us to deliver our services? What observations/ questions have they been sharing?*

Q– *What additional information would be useful?*

Note: To avoid having questions like this one lead to wasted time, effort, and expense, first play the *"Let's pretend we have that information; what will we do with it?"* game. If no one can clearly identify how this information will be utilized other than as a door stop, paper weight, or justification for two more servers in the server farm, don't pursue the information.

Q– *What do you see as significant opportunities?*

- Narrow or expand our mission?
- Redefine the appropriate audiences?
- Increase/reduce/modify _____?
- Re-brand?
- Concentrate resources/effort?

Q– *How can we enhance our communications to potential clients to:*

- Assure expectations match delivery?
- Services deliver desired outcomes?

The "get-to" approaches described above are about creating cultures of valued leadership. Remember, an organization's culture is about the collective practices of every stakeholder in the organization. And to have a culture of valued leadership, every stakeholder **gets-to** bring leadership thought to the organization.

"Get-to" approaches lead to openness, creativity, and entrepreneurial thinking.

Try This Exercise

When I hear someone say—during a radio or television interview, a webcast, or TED Talk—**"We need to"** or **"We must,"** I mentally substitute the phrase **"We get to"** or **"We have the opportunity to."** This change always feels positive. It expands my thinking. It makes me smile. And it moves me to ponder opportunities.

Try it. Think of it as an exercise program to develop your valued leadership skills.

"Get-to" beats "Got-to" is not just a title for this chapter. It is a catalyst to expand your leadership thinking and contributions.

Chapter 5

Labels. Move Past Them.

We humans have a fondness for labels. And we seem to have a natural talent for labeling. Labels work effectively for computer files and physical files for desk drawers. The label narrows our focus so related materials can be easily stored and retrieved.

When we label people and ideas, we not only narrow our focus, we narrow our perspectives, openness, and receptivity. Labels become attached to beliefs, biases, and "facts" which may or may not be factual.

In our society, and I assume in every society, people tend to label each other. We label our practices, our beliefs, even our mannerisms. We place others and ourselves into groups by using labels. And we attach our personal shades of negative or positive perspectives to the person or thing labeled.

Although labels really do not tell us a lot about the person or idea, we pretend they do. For example, a parent's discipline of his or her child is observed. Someone describes the interaction and labels it as "old-fashioned" (whatever that means). It is then an easy leap for that label to be attached to the parent as though all their parenting interactions will be "old-fashioned." It is also easy to make the next leap that this label will be an accurate description of all aspects of this person's life. The label diminishes our capacity to observe. The label, at least initially, suppresses or increases both our desire and ability to interact with that person.

The composite of attachments we give to the label tend to:

- Influence and often diminish our capacity to explore possibilities.
- Inhibit the breath and quality of interactions.
- Inhibit our collective capacity to surface fresh ideas, strategies, and tactics.

The Danish philosopher Kierkegaard is credited with the following quote:

"Once you label me, you negate me."

And it seems to me that *once we label each other, we diminish our capacity to hear and be heard.*

This reality is easy to observe in the context of political discussions. Once ideas, problems, or even potential solutions are labeled as conservative, progressive, or liberal, the capacity for collective effort and innovative thought is diminished.

Listen to political discourse. Rather than take sides and root for your home team, i.e., your preferred label, be a student of the discourse. Notice how quickly labels surface and how quickly your personal reactions surface in response. Notice how your reactions impact your capacity to listen. Notice how participants tend to move to their comfortable corners in the town square of ideas. Observe how frequently you hear a "we must" statement.

Although participants indicate they want to solve X, Y or Z, the labels diminish their capacity to do so. The "post-label" dialogue and editorial-oriented monologues tend to focus on each labeled side pointing out the other labeled side's misguided assumptions and conclusions about the workings of the real world. The labels diminish participants' capacity to exchange ideas, identify opportunities, define desired outcomes, or even initiate a next step.

Labels Heard Inside Organizations

Labels surface quickly in discussions within organizations. These labels tend to focus on functions, specializations and hierarchy. As with other labels, people attach their perceptions, beliefs, and "facts." The consequences may be less obvious than those heard in political settings but they are no less impactful to the dynamics of organizations.

Once a label is used, notice how quickly your personal reactions surface and how your reactions impact your capacity to listen. Notice how participants tend to move to their comfortable corners in the organizational town square of ideas. Observe how frequently you hear a version of a 'we-must' phrase.

Function and specialization labels include such terms as marketing, sales, finance, human relations, and the ever popular IT. Interesting that technology gets the "it" label when no one seems to know what "it" is. See how easy it was for me to assign bias to a label? I just attached an obstacle to working with these folks. And I did it in just one sentence.

Functional areas can easily become "silos" of separation. You know silos exist in an organization when you hear endearing references such as:

- *"Those _____ people."* (Insert your silo of choice. Just for fun, you can also attach one of your favorite adjectives. And, please, do not pretend you have not done this many times.)

- *"They are the ones who have to do _____ before we can do _____. And you cannot even begin to get them involved without begging."*

- *"You can't make a move without them."*

- *"They are the people who keep anything from getting done around here."*

It is likely that you can hear additional fun phrases like these being shared during "happy-hour" celebrations.

Once a person is labeled as a member of the (fill in the blank) department, people make assumptions about that person's baseline of knowledge, skills, and capacity to add value. These assumptions may have evolved from past work encounters—positive or negative—or from invalid information about the department or person. The more individuals are identified by their organizational label, the deeper the challenge to leverage collective intelligence and ingenuity.

Although the dynamics of organizational labels can be complex, here is a simple situation that demonstrates how easily labels impact interactions.

Let's say you are the designated leader of a project group. Your group is comprised of people who have worked together previously. You need to introduce an "outsider" who is joining the group. Your introduction, although a simple thing, can contribute to genuine welcoming, and the team moves on. Or it can lead to significant wasted energy, i.e., "Prove it, sister" attitudes.

Look at these three introductions, exaggerated for effect:

- **Introduction 1**: *This is Jane. We have to include her on our project because the powers that be say we have to include someone from the _____ department or they will not sign off for us to move forward.* (Ok, so you likely will not say this exactly this way unless you just had your budget cut, the dog ate your handouts, or your favorite team lost their big game.)

- **Introduction 2**: *This is Jane. She works in the _____ department. She has been assigned to our project team.* (Wow— this will generate a rousing round of positive enthusiasm.

- **Introduction 3 (no labels)**: *Let me introduce Jane. I asked if she could join our project team because she has terrific skills to help us _____. I had an opportunity to work with her on _____. She helped that group quickly learn to use the software that we will use on our group's project. We would not have been able to accomplish what we did as efficiently as we did without her assistance.* (Warning: Focus on how she contributed and avoid over-the-top praise. Otherwise, her associates will dump the entire project on her, hack into her resume, post it on a *lookingforajob.com* site, and tell her supervisor that she is seeking new employment.)

Small events like this introduction scenario occur frequently in every organization. They present opportunities to contribute to, or avoid, the baggage of labels. Prepare for and utilize these opportunities.

Hierarchy Labels

Organizations have multiple levels of expectations, authority, and accountability. A variety of labels designate who, at least in theory, resides at these levels. People then attach their perceptions, beliefs, and facts (accurate or not), to these labels. These attachments are influenced by the actions of previous people who held the title, the current title holder's pronouncements during their first meetings with their underlings, and daily interactions.

Examples of these labels include:

- Supervisor, Manager, Department Head, Vice-President of Wow, Senior Vice-President of Something That Sounds Important
- President, CEO
- Team/Project Leader
- Subordinates, Direct Reports

Informal references to hierarchy labels include:

- Boss
- Head Dude or Duchess
- Person in charge
- The all-knowing wise one
- A noun preceded by a string of positive or negative adjectives
- Valued leader

Hierarchy labels do serve a purpose. They help determine who to throw insults toward when things go badly. They provide titles to print on business cards and resumes. And, of course, they do at least partially define roles and responsibilities. I am not campaigning that they be eliminated. I am campaigning that we acknowledge that they are labels, and labels can diminish our capacity to interact in healthy ways.

Labeling Markets

Today's technology enables people to be placed into increasingly tightly-defined groupings so products, services, and delivery methods can be positioned for marketing and sales initiatives. Social media facilitates both the positioning and execution of these initiatives. The world has gotten very skilled at this. But remember Kierkegaard's quote, "Once you label me, you negate me."

If you are engaged in selling stuff, it is easy to miss opportunities once you assign a label to potential clients. For example, let's say you have the credentials to assist people in the selection and purchase of financial products.

Based on information you were provided or acquired, you label your prospective clients as "a young, suburban, dual income couple with 2.2 children and 1.3 pets." Once this description or label is assigned, you begin to make assumptions about the couple's likely combination of income, debt, investment capacity, need for various kinds and amounts of insurance, etc.

If you proceed based on your set of assumptions about the "labeled" client, you will limit your potential to provide the client with multiple services both immediately and over time.

This same labeling dynamic can arise when organizations are labeled. They might become labeled by their broader industry (energy, manufacturing, technology), or by their structure (partnership, publicly traded corporation, LLC), or by their business phase (entrepreneurial start-up, rapidly expanding, mature). Think of the labels you use frequently. Every label can diminish your capacity to listen, observe, and learn. They can diminish your capacity to surface opportunities.

Successful professionals overcome the limitation of labels. They know that moving past labels opens possibilities. Moving past labels will surface opportunities for valued leadership.

Move past the labels. Focus on opportunities.

Chapter 6

People Want to Play. Let Them.

Some organizations conduct exhaustive research to select strategies and tactics. Some wing it rather than research it. Some jump on the bandwagon of ideas that magically surface. Some spend big bucks to bring in a touted guru available on this year's version of *"It's a Miracle Strategy"* traveling circus. Regardless of origin, the strategies selected will ultimately find their place on this strategy continuum:

Obviously, you want to utilize strategies that end up on the right side of this continuum. But before you exhaust the fuel in your search engine tank looking for the perfect strategy, consider this one:

Engage the composite talents of your people.

This strategy will:

- Enhance associates' knowledge of their organization and industry.
- Reinforce creativity, innovation, and entrepreneurial thinking.
- Identify people ready for new opportunities.
- Create advocates for the organization.
- Allow associates to have some fun.

If this sounds a little over the top and you feel like muttering "give me a break," then go ahead. Mutter away. You will feel better.

Let's look at how a strategy evolved that engaged the talents of associates at one organization and reinforced a culture of valued leadership.

As often happens, this strategy was not some preconceived masterpiece. Rather it evolved from the collective energy of associates who became involved. Of course, the associates had to first become interested and willing to be involved. The tactic used to generate interest was a show-and-tell experience. The energy to create the show-and-tell came from a couple of associates who were irritated with the current situation.

These comments summarize their irritation: *"Our 'stuff' does not look as good as our competitor's 'stuff.' Our materials are outdated, inconsistent, and confusing. We can't stand it any longer; we have to do something."*

Their initial goal was to get other associates to accept the idea that there were multiple opportunities to take action so our 'stuff' represents us better in the marketplace.

To create the show-and-tell, the people most riled up about this issue gathered samples of every printed or electronic brochure, business processing form, and support resource. These samples were displayed on and around a large conference table. The display enabled viewers to easily see appearance, messaging, and branding inconsistencies. It became obvious why so much frustration about business forms was expressed openly and often. It also was obvious why forms-training was required and, even after the training, forms were still improperly completed.

After the initial rounds of self-ridicule grew tiresome, folks began to be **students** of what they were seeing. They studied the design differences and identified missing ingredients, inconsistent messaging, and points of confusion. Their observations eventually evolved into a checklist of do's and don'ts for future pieces.

Next Step- Showtime for the Bigs

The "irritated but excited to make a difference folks" invited members of senior management to view the display. To add a little spice to the display, they created some large expense-data charts. After all, everyone knows that members of senior management (there I go labeling again) can always get worked into an absolute frenzy when they see expense trend lines go up.

The display and data were compelling. When Mr. Big asked, *"What do you propose we do about all this?,"* the show-and-tell team was ready to propose specific "next steps." These next steps did not reflect leadership genius but they did keep the ball rolling. The ultimate larger organizational development idea was still evolving from the reactions to these initial show and tell experiences.

Of course, since multiple people in multiple silos created all the stuff, the "opportunity" (i.e., extra work required) to enhance the stuff would have to be "sold" to the people in the silos.

Next Step- Involve The Silos

The unofficial leaders of this effort (the irritated ones) asked senior management to invite one person from each business unit (the silos) to view the display, hear the information, and join a task force to pursue these objectives:

- Achieve some "quick wins."
- Reduce expenses by eliminating duplication and obsolete items.
- Create a consistent look and feel for client facing resources.
- Assure each piece becomes a component of a system (sales process, client service model, etc.) and is appropriately integrated into the bigger picture of the organization.

Seeing Bigger Opportunities

This assignment was easy to grasp and it did generate some quick wins. The observations of task force participants became more insightful. Initially, questions focused on things like fonts (once everyone learned what a font was) and where the company name and logo needed to be placed. Then, the observations and questions progressed toward **purpose and effectiveness**. People asked why each resource existed. They asked about "desired outcomes." They asked if the story being told was meaningful. They pondered whether different resources could generate enhanced client experiences.

The initial source of irritation, *"our stuff did not look as good as our competitor's stuff,"* had inspired people to think about opportunities rather than just quick fixes. Associates were enhancing their understanding of their business model. They were gaining an appreciation for each other's knowledge, skills, perspectives, and the realities of their individual areas of responsibilities. And as they enhanced their skills to observe the bigger picture, they challenged each other to ask better "why" and "how does this fit into our system" questions.

So, with this foundation in place, the next challenge was to create a tactic that could:

- Sustain people's interest and involvement.
- Generate value for each person contributing their time and leadership.
- Expand the benefits to more areas of the organization.
- Be easily utilized by all participants.

The "Next Level" Tactic

The tactic created evolved from the participants' interactions. Those interactions evidenced that everyone was looking for a way to pull things together. Here is the tactic that was created. Each participant was asked to create *timelines of touchpoints* for each group of stakeholders impacted by their area. For example, the **touchpoint** sequence for prospective clients might begin with an advertisement, a brochure, or a web page. The next touchpoint might be a phone conversation. Subsequent touchpoints might include an initial fact-finding interview, a sales presentation, completion of business applications, confirmation of order, delivery of product, post-sale communications, etc. Participants were also asked to insert what they felt could be new touchpoints that did not currently exist but could become valuable enhancements to the client experience.

The term **"touchpoint"** was intentionally used. It raised awareness that resources—their messaging and their delivery—create positive, zero, or negative impact. It challenged participants to think in terms of enhanced connections and "desired outcomes" rather than "let's fix some stuff."

The **timeline** approach enabled people to think bigger picture. Because participants were viewing the entire stakeholder experience, they were asking better questions and identifying better ideas. Participants moved from "get it off my to-do list" thinking to "let's capture opportunities" thinking.

Who were the **stakeholder groups**? They were any group of people who had an interest in the organization's success. These groups included: prospective clients, existing clients, employees, sales representatives, managers, corporate shareholders, corporate boards of directors, and vendors.

Separate timelines were created for newer as well as long time clients, sales representatives, and employees. Why? Because this approach enabled participants to spot opportunities that could enhance the experiences of these very different groups.

This **"touchpoint, timeline"** tactic became the common framework that all current and future participants in this process could grasp and explain. You might be wondering why these people, who were already fully busy doing their jobs, were willing to use this tactic and participate in this effort. The answer is that the preamble of the **shared experiences** of viewing resources and participating in critique sessions provided evidence that the organization was open to and welcoming of leadership thought. Without these shared experiences it is doubtful that the above tactic, or any tactic introduced, would have been embraced.

Creating a culture where leadership thought and action is considered normal behavior relies on consistency of experience. The shared experience of creating timelines prepared everyone to share observations and ask questions. The shared interactions helped identify overlooked touchpoints as well as potential new ones. Participants quickly recognized that every touchpoint was an opportunity to deliver a quality experience.

The following questions were used to evaluate the "substance" of each touchpoint:

- What is the purpose/desired outcome?
- Are desired outcomes being achieved?
- Does it promote desired professional image and reputation?
- Does it attract, retain, and positively reinforce the stakeholder?
- Does synergy result within its family of touchpoints?
- Does it ease the burden of administration (reduce cost, errors)?
- Does it simplify or eliminate need for training?
- Is it cost justified?

These questions identified opportunities to reduce, consolidate, and enhance resources. More importantly, they fostered conversations that enabled people to become more connected personally and professionally. They broke down barriers. They reinforced a culture where leadership of thought was encouraged.

Sustaining the Project

What began as a visual examination of "stuff" progressed into an impactful engagement of people. People gained insights about the business. Their leadership of thought was positively reinforced. They made positive contributions. Therefore, the process was sustained. New people joined the task force. Some experienced members moved on but replaced themselves with people whom they wanted to represent their turf. **People wanted to play.**

This process sustained itself for eight years. It facilitated multiple advancements for the organization. It was the catalyst to many spin-off projects. And because people already had the background knowledge, they did not need to be "sold," i.e., convinced to lend a hand. They already grasped the opportunity and were willing to move forward.

People engaged in this process moved into more meaningful roles of organizational leadership. Because of their shared experiences, they had been schooled in receptivity to new ideas. They were open to the concept that people want to play on the organization's playground. They were in positions to continue to reinforce a culture where openness of leadership thought was welcomed.

And importantly, because they had **opportunities to listen and learn,** they could **teach and coach.**

So Do You Engage Your People Talent or Not?

Perhaps, after reviewing all this information, your inner voice is saying some version of, *"Nice theory, but really, given my visionary leadership and superior communication skills–by the way, did you know I majored in psychology and minored in communications at a prestigious college—anyway, my people are thrilled with my leadership. They know exactly where I want to take my organization. They do not want to waste each other's time listening to goofy leadership ideas. We have a leader. It's me. My people just need to get on with it to implement my vision."*

If that is what your inner Yoda is whispering to you, I offer this thought for you to ponder. If you are receiving all the value you can tolerate from your associates; if you have implemented all the innovations they could create; if your newer and experienced people are fully engaged; if your reputation in your industry is all it can be; if everyone is enamored with your leadership awesomeness; and if you do not want to be annoyed by insights or suggestions, then close this book and just get on with it. Justice and the American way will be served. *Business Week* and *Rolling Stone* magazines await your willingness to bless them with interviews. And the rest of us will look forward to your soon-to-be-announced TED Talk.

If, however, all these things are not occurring, **identify an opportunity to let your people play.**

We just examined how one organization leveraged a point of irritation into a larger organizational development strategy. The visual display and creation of touchpoint timelines proved to be effective tactics. The visual display provided evidence of the need. The timelines provided enhanced understanding of the business model. Both generated sufficient curiosity to keep people engaged.

These tactics may or may not be meaningful to your organization. If they are, use them to get started. If not, every organization has opportunities to engage the knowledge, skills and interests of their people in new ways.

How do you identify these opportunities? **Listen and Learn.** When you hear yourself or others say, *"I wish we had...It would be better if we could...If we had xyz in place we could stop wasting time on...What if we could...Why don't we stop...,"* you have found a potential **opportunity to reinforce a culture of valued leadership**. Don't waste time looking for a perfect opportunity. Just identify one that has the desired ingredients. These questions will help you identify an opportunity:

Q– Do people have significant energy—positive or negative—about the problem or "desired outcome"?

Q– Will resolution of this problem be significant to the organization? To determine significance, assume the issue is resolved. List resulting benefits. Then answer this question: Do these benefits position our organization to pursue new opportunities?

Q– Does the issue have broad-based relevance?

Q– Will meaningful progress require multiple "silos" of knowledge and skills to resolve?

Q– Is the issue a symptom of a larger challenge? If so, that is a good thing. It can become a catalyst to examine more impactful initiatives.

Q– Can potential "quick wins" be identified? Quick wins build enthusiasm and advocacy for the project.

Once an opportunity is identified you can proceed with these steps:

- Identify the advocates (people passionate about the issue).
- Identify/share potential benefits.
- Coach the advocates to:
  - *Listen and learn.*
  - *Identify "desired outcomes."*
  - *Play the "What If We Succeed?" game. What difference did we make?*
  - *Identify "quick wins."*
  - *Strengthen their case.*
  - *Create an opening event, i.e., "conference room display".*
- Identify key people in the organization who will likely have little interest for this opportunity but will ultimately need to contribute (or at least not obstruct). Do not pretend they do not exist.
- Identify additional knowledge/skills/resources needed to be successful.
- Identify the facilitators/champions to advance the project. Ideal candidates:
  - *Possess organizational credibility.*
  - *Are genuinely curious.*
  - *Are not glory hounds.*

We started this chapter with the observation that dynamic organizations continuously strive to improve. To do so they employ a wide range of strategies. The questions and steps above will enable you to identify opportunities to engage your people. Those opportunities will lead to new sources of valued leadership.

Let Them Play.

Now, let's examine a vital ingredient for cultures of valued leadership. Clarity.

Chapter 7

Clarity. Both an Opportunity and a Responsibility

Let's face reality. It is hard to deliver clarity. We intend for our messages to be clear, but frequently hear ourselves saying *"Well, what I really meant was_____."*

Let's say you have the responsibility to inform others about an organizational initiative, policy change, meeting, or project. The facts (time, place, participants) are easy to communicate. The context (answering the "why" questions and providing background and perspective) is not so easy to communicate.

Providing the context is where **clarity meets leadership opportunity.** It is where we engage leadership thinking rather than messenger thinking. These leadership opportunities arise not just in the context of major announcements and presentations. They also arise through the flow of daily messages, memos, and 90 percent of every power point presentation I have ever seen.

Let's just view these opportunities as a game. We can name it, *Clarity: A Game of Leadership*.

Desired results of the game:

- Communications that communicate.
- Reputation for clarity.
- Valued leadership.

Playing the Game

Unless your communication is a text message or a simple reminder about an upcoming meeting, the hardest part of composing clear communication is getting started. So to get started:

- Make a list of information you may want to include.
- Don't slow down to judge each item. If it comes to mind, add it to the list.
- Glance at recently received or sent messages to prompt your thinking.

> **Helpful idea:** Create a file of messages you receive that succeed in grabbing your attention. These will be a source of ideas for your future messages.

Now, go to the top of your list and add these three items:

1. Desired Outcomes.

2. Opportunities.

3. Valued Leadership.

For every message, ask yourself *"What are my 'desired outcomes?'"* By answering this question, you will not only enrich your message, you will anticipate the likely "next steps."

Every message presents opportunities to achieve more than just delivery of the facts. One significant opportunity, always present yet easily neglected, is **consistency.** Consistency strengthens organizations.

Consistency increases the confidence and trust of individuals so they can strengthen their organization. Consistency enables valued leadership to be delivered. Here are other opportunities to consider. You can:

- "Position" the message in a larger context.
- Offer encouragement, reinforcement, and recognition.
- Share appreciation and congratulations.
- Offer assistance and coaching.
- Share metrics that show progress.
- Solicit feedback and ideas.
- Share potential "next steps."

Messages are opportunities to demonstrate valued leadership. Occasionally messages are of the big deal variety (sometimes referred to as "Wow" items.) More frequently they are of the not-a-big-deal variety (sometimes referred to as "Yeah, whatever" items). Regardless of variety, by including **Valued Leadership** on your list of things to include, you will expand your thinking to encompass tone, style, perspective, and respect. And you will remember to *"First, do no harm."*

These sunny-side up observations do not in any way imply that difficult messages are being avoided. Discipline, toughness, and forthrightness are all elements of valued leadership. So even if you are the head shed duchess or dude and you get to say whatever you want in whatever way you want, reflecting on the **Valued Leadership** concept will lead you to capture the opportunities from even the most difficult messages.

Drafting Your Message

Now that you have expanded your list of items, you can start hitting the key board to compose your message. Here are some hints:

- Fewer words trump more words.
- Shorter sentences trump longer ones.
- Phrases trump sentences.
- Lists trump long sentences and long paragraphs.
- Concise summaries of reference documents trump attachments.

Also, don't drive yourself to distraction trying to compose the perfect *"It was the best of times, it was the worst of times..."* opening.[1] If it makes you happy, you can edit yourself into the annals of great works of organizational literature later. This is not about perfect writing or prose. Few of us are capable of and/or patient enough to deliver on that level. From my perspective, people would rather have your message cut to the chase than read a short story regardless of how well it is written.

If you want to start your message by saying thanks, then type *"Thanks."* Then share why you are saying thanks. If your message is about an upcoming event just type, *"On Thursday, May 3, at 8:00 a.m., we will begin our annual Managers Conference."* And away you go. Again, don't slow down searching for perfect words or phrases. Just keep going.

You will likely create some long sentences and paragraphs. They can be repackaged for clarity. Here's how. Read what you have written. Find the end of your introductory thought, plunk in your keyboard curser, and hit the **enter key**. You have started a new paragraph or an initial item for a list.

---

1 "It was the best of times, it was the worst of times, it was the age of wisdom, it was the age of foolishness, it was the epoch of belief, it was the epoch of incredulity, it was the season of Light, it was the season of Darkness, it was the spring of hope, it was the winter of despair..."
– Charles Dickens, *A Tale of Two Cities* (1859)

If it is to be a list, hit the **hyphen key**...the **enter key**...the **tab key**. Your first bulleted item is now under your opening commentary. Find the beginning of the next piece of information. Hit the **enter key**. Magically, you have a second bullet. Continue this until you have divided all the pieces of related information into a list.

The list format makes it easy to spot what you have included and what is missing. It makes it easy to reduce the number of words and reduce sentences to phrases. It makes it easy for you to cut and paste to enhance the flow and move what does not belong in this list into a separate section of your message. Quickly, you will have surrounded your total message. You can then finesse the look and feel.

Look at the following example. First, you see the version that conveys that the sender has a lot of material to share and wants people to receive it. The revised version conveys that the sender has a lot of material to share, wants people to receive it, and wants to respect the recipients' time by providing useful context and clarity. The latter approach better enables recipients to ask questions and offer feedback. It enhances the sender's reputation for clarity.

Version 1:

Hey all, I have some thoughts and suggestions for you concerning the communications for our upcoming event. I know you have already done some work on this but I want to assure you have the benefit of my perspectives and expectations. I also want to make sure that you have a complete strategy and set of tactics that will increase attention and interest while we also positively reinforce our brand in this space. So here are a few of my ideas and suggestions. Let's do a series of messages and keep them consistent and soundly worded so people can easily spot the important elements. Then also add attachments and include the multiple ways they can contact us to get more information and sign up to attend. I think we can find multiple lists we can use and you will want, of course, to customize the message for each list. And while we are at it let's be sure to capture the contact information from the people contacted so we can keep dripping information on them. Don't forget that we want to let everyone know that we have lots of experience offering these programs and they will benefit from attending. Perhaps we can also ask them to forward our message to others on their distribution lists who they think would benefit from our program. I know you folks are working hard on improving the results over our last event. I know you have other priorities to complete but this event is also important so do not let your other work get in the way of bringing good efforts to this project. And I want you to be sure to think outside the box. You can do some research to find what others are doing and add those to our mix. We are always open to new ideas and new methods. Thanks for letting me share. I look forward to you making our event a success and then you can proceed to your other assignments. I appreciate your attention. Let me know if you want to discuss my ideas further. I will look forward to an update soon on the new things you are adding and the results you are achieving. I hope my thoughts are clear and I think some of these ideas can make a difference.

Metrics: 386 words; 21 sentences; 1 paragraph. Odds of being read: Slim.

Did I exaggerate this version just for fun? Yes. But do not pretend you have not drafted or received messages almost as confusing and irritating. Here is another version.

Version 2:

Joe, Karen and Louise, Thanks for yesterday's update.

You asked for ideas. Here they are. You may have already considered most of them. If not, I hope they are helpful.

*Generate a **series** of features- benefits- logistics messages:*

> ▶ ***Deadlines** for discounts for **Exclusive Experience**.*

> • *Sell benefits of the features.*

> ▶ *Enrollment/ payment instructions.*

- ▶ *Reinforce our brand and value - create identity for components - examples:*
  - *"**Masters Coaching**"- Main platform presentations.*
  - *"**Extra Dialogue**" workshops.*
  - *"**Distance Learning - Diagnostics for Progress**" seminars.*
  - *"**Connections to Mentors**" post program offerings.*

- ▶ *Potential **contact lists**:*
  - *Past graduates*
  - *Professional society members*
  - *City and Regional affiliates*

- ▶ ***Capture contact info:***
  - *Enrollees - series of messages to sell benefits and heighten interest.*
  - *Contacts not yet enrolled - allow option to continue to receive updates.*

- ▶ *Post event **thank-you** notes - gather **suggestions.***

Again, thanks for the update. I appreciate how effectively you all shared the information. You are succeeding in exciting the entire organization about this program.

Thanks for your leadership.

Metrics: 154 words; 9 sentences; 4 lists; 23 bold-faced words. Odds of being read: High.

Will it take a little more time to create version two than version one? Perhaps, but practice will help you become proficient. To practice just find a lengthy message you either received or sent recently. Copy the message into a new document. Then create a new, more concise version.

Here are some additional suggestions to help you generate messages that both provide clarity and value.

Before Sending Your Message, consider the following:

▶ *Set your drafted message aside. Reread later. Revise.*

▶ *For "Big Deal" (organizational rioting could be provoked) messages, get objective feedback before hitting "send."*

▶ *Assume "other people" will read the message. If sending to:*

- Sales team - Assume clients read it.

- Supervisors - Assume those being supervised read it.

▶ *Ask yourself:*

- **Q–** *If "other people" read the message, would they feel respected?*

- **Q–** *If I received this message, would I:*
  - ○ *Easily grasp why I received it?*
  - ○ *Appreciate receiving it?*
  - ○ *Have the information I need and know what to do?*

- **Q–** *If your family, competitors, peers, boss, bigger boss or "Saturday Night Live" skit writers read it, will you be proud?*

▶ *If your emotions are screaming such thoughts as, "I am going to put a stop to this… I am going to put those people in their place…I will show them what is important and what is not," ask yourself:*

- **Q–** What are my desired outcomes?

- **Q–** Will my message deliver valued leadership?

Admit it. Many of the messages you receive can be a source of entertainment. You and your pals get to joke with each other about what the messenger really wanted to say. But do you want your messages to be seen in that context? Of course you do not.

Clarity is the responsibility of a valued leader. The clarity you provide will foster opportunity thinking plus convey that you have the ability to coach and mentor.

Your efforts will demostrate and reinforce a culture of valued leadership.

Chapter 8

Today We Will Discuss...

We are all guilty of beginning meetings by saying, *"We are here to discuss . . ."* or *"Today we will talk about . . ."* Why? What's wrong with us? Don't we have better things to do than pull together a bunch of talented people and just discuss stuff?

Such an opening might be appropriate for your local book club gathering (although I would suggest a more meaningful opening will generate more interest and better discussion). For other meetings, the "we will discuss" opening can easily zap the positive energy that people brought to the meeting. On the plus side, if treats are being provided, people have more time to enjoy them.

Whether you are professor of the class, moderator of the meeting, or even Mr. or Ms. I'm-In-Charge, beginning the gathering with a "Today we will discuss . . ." phrase will not provide clarity, generate enthusiasm, or create an expectation of meaningful outcomes.

In the absence of a specific purpose, the void will be filled with distractions, tangents, and passive-aggressive behavior. Surely we can identify and describe a higher purpose for our gathering.

Valued leadership provides a purpose for gatherings of organizational talent. The purpose could be: *"Today we will . . . reach a decision on .*

. . identify our gaps in . . . identify the criteria on which a vendor will be evaluated . . . select our vendor."

Are the people invited to these events actually going to discuss stuff? Yes, of course. But when the meeting begins with a specific statement of purpose, the discussions can quickly focus on that purpose. If you are the leader of the meeting, ask yourself these questions:

Q– Why have I asked these people to meet? What are the desired outcomes?

Q– How will I succinctly present this purpose so participants are immediately engaged?

Q– What opportunities can be captured during the meeting?

By the way, if you cannot answer these questions, postpone the meeting.

If you are not the designated leader of a meeting you can still add value by respectfully asking a version of, "What are we wanting to accomplish today?" Everyone involved will appreciate being "in the know."

Providing such clarity is evidence of a culture of valued leadership.

Chapter 9
Power of Our Professional Beliefs

"We take a handful of sand from the endless landscape of awareness around us and call that handful of sand the world."
—Zen and The Art of Motorcycle Maintenance, *Robert Pirsig.*

I underlined the above sentence when I read it many years ago. I love the image. I love the message. And I enjoy sharing it with people engaged in professional development activities. In a few words, the quote conveys how easily we limit our awareness and therefore see no need to pick up a few more grains of knowledge, skills, and insights.

Some of the grains we pick up evolve into our professional beliefs. These beliefs are just as powerful as are our beliefs about parenting, exercising, spirituality, religion, and, of course, fishing lures. Our professional beliefs—valid or invalid, recognized or unrecognized, constructive or limiting—shape both our potential for results and our actual results. These beliefs can be catalysts for change or obstacles to change. They can help us listen and learn, or diminish our capacity to do either.

I have witnessed thousands of interactions where people agreed and disagreed with others about their professional points of view and business practices. The stronger the beliefs, the more animated the interpersonal dynamics. Faces sometimes turned red. Words sometimes turned blue. Those dynamics naturally impacted their organization's dynamics.

Here's an interaction I observed during a panel discussion. Actually I have seen variations of this interaction many times concerning many subjects. The subject of this day was recruiting and selecting candidates who would become successful within the business model of being independent entrepreneurs. Panelist A expressed the belief (he, of course, did not use that word) that people without previous experience in business could not be successful in this role. His actual comments sounded like, *"It is a waste of my and my team's time to bring someone on board who has not had at least five years of related business experience. People without that experience simply cannot grasp the demands or the opportunities of this position."* Panelist B expressed the belief (she, of course, did not use that word) that she could absolutely recruit and select people with no previous business experience and coach them to success. Her comments sounded like, *"I came into this business without experience. I have made many people who had no experience successful. I enjoy making this happen."* The unsaid, yet implied, message was, *"I am just a better leader."*

What began as a light-hearted and witty exchange between two very successful leaders evolved into a heated argument. Unfortunately, they were both so focused on proving they were right that the audience did not benefit from learning about the tactics each of them used to coach people to success. The panelists merely validated their beliefs. They did not seek to listen and learn.

Let me share a few more examples of professional beliefs. As you read these statements, begin each one with the words, ***I believe*** or ***I know:***

> *... that even though I am overwhelmed by all the things I have to do, I cannot rely on others to get things done the way I want them done.*

> *... that I cannot recruit the people I really want because they are not likely to be successful in our business model.*

... that I came into this business with an entrepreneurial mindset. No one helped me be successful. The people I recruit can only succeed if they do the same.

... I need to keep people accountable but I can't because I need the "body count" to make my required recruiting numbers.

... our readiness process is just a bunch of stuff we have people do. They can do this stuff on their own without my guidance or involvement.

I am guessing you may have expected loftier examples of professional beliefs. Perhaps you had in mind beliefs about span of control, opportunity costs, or the "Five Absolutes of Effective Leadership." There are lots of those professional beliefs being carried around. I shared the above more pragmatic beliefs because they are examples of ones that impact our thinking and our tactics. They are examples of beliefs that can be readily examined, modified, retained, or replaced.

Glance back at the above list of beliefs. Then ask yourself:

- **Q–** What if these beliefs were modified or replaced?
- **Q–** What if new business tactics were engaged around these new beliefs?
- **Q–** Would those new tactics have a significant impact on future outcomes?

Now read the following different versions of the previous list. Again, begin each one with the words, *I believe* or *I know:*

...I do not have the skill or capacity to do everything, and I know I will accomplish more by recruiting, training, and retaining a support team.

... I can coach new associates to be successful.

> *... that, although I succeeded in this business without a lot of guidance, I can coach others who have an entrepreneurial mindset to become successful faster because of the lessons I learned.*

> *... when I help people hold themselves accountable, their level of success is higher.*

> *... that, by personally coaching candidates through my readiness process, they and I can make a jointly agreed upon, quality business decision about whether to continue in this career.*

As you compare these two lists you may be inclined to see one as invalid and the other as valid. That is not the intent. These are merely examples of differing beliefs. Each of us carries around professional beliefs, recognized or not, that impact our practices and our outcomes.

My perspectives about organizations being **cultures of valued leadership** reflect my professional beliefs. Here are a few I carry around. *I believe:*

- *...everyone wants to play, to contribute. And if they do not get that opportunity, the organization loses good talent or, worse, talented people stay but seek non-productive ways to be acknowledged.*

- *...people have talent that they have not yet begun to utilize.*

- *...many people have the talent to be mentors and are not given that opportunity.*

- *...we carry around professional beliefs, recognized or not, that inhibit our success.*

- *...for an organization to become great, it must both teach and learn.*

- *...the better organizations are at creating cultures of valued leadership versus just **the** leaders being valued, the more they receive their associates' best efforts.*

- *...life is far too short to allow our valuable time to be spent in environments where we do not get to play.*

What are the professional beliefs you carry around? Are they limiting you or creating opportunities?

It is a challenge to identify our professional beliefs. It is a bigger challenge to view them objectively. Recognize these challenges as opportunities and you will have taken the initial step toward objectivity.

Examining Your Professional Beliefs

Here is an idea you can use to gain additional objectivity. Ask your mentor for feedback. If you do not have a mentor, this is a perfect way to initiate such a relationship. You can use the following words to request that assistance:

"In handling my duties, I have been assuming that_____ is true. My tactics have been based on that assumption. I am not sure my assumption is accurate and it may be limiting my results. I would appreciate your input. Ask me some questions; give me your feedback."

Some of your professional beliefs are serving you well. Some are not. Acknowledge that you have them. Examine them. Seek input. Then decide whether to retain, modify, or replace them.

Awareness and understanding of your professional beliefs impacts your ability to deliver valued leadership.

Want to pick up many more grains of awareness and understanding about the impact of your professional beliefs? You can do so by studying the book, *Mindset: The New Psychology of Success,* by Carol Dweck, Ph.D.[2] The author's research-driven observations offer great information and perspectives about the power of beliefs. This book will also provide great food for thought concerning your conversations with your children and grandchildren.

2 *Mindset: The New Psychology of Success,* Carol S. Dweck, Ph.D. Copyright 2006, Publisher, Random House. ISBN 978-0-345-47232-8.

Chapter 10- Selecting Talent
The Fog of Competency

"In cultures of valued leadership competency thrives and progression from one level to the next is celebrated."

Let's say your organization has an ***opportunity*** to add staff, create a new department, or initiate a significant project. Notice I used the word "opportunity" rather than the word "need." It is natural to refer to such opportunities in terms of need. We plead our case with statements like, *We need to get more help... If you do not get me some help, I am going to go crazy or give up... Who can we get to do this stuff that is beneath my dignity and keeping me from doing what I was born to do?* Ok, so the last one is only shared with the mirror during your morning rituals of preparing for your day.

Regardless of such pre-caffeine morning mutterings, let's agree to engage the **professional belief** that these **"needs" are opportunities**. When viewed in this context, we can expand our own and our associates' professional thinking.

For example, the **opportunity** to add someone new to your organization is about more than just determining if candidates can do the job. The opportunity is about:

- Engaging the candidate's **unique composite of knowledge, skills, and competencies** in your organization.
- Creating **synergy within the ensemble of existing talent** in the organization.
- Reinforcing **openness to new possibilities.**

Assume you submitted a proposal for a new associate and it has been approved. You now get to:

- Refine the **position's description**—purpose, objectives, responsibilities, activities.
- Determine the **eligibility requirements**—knowledge, skills, experience.
- Identify types and levels of desired **competencies.**
- Engage a *culture of valued leadership* **selection process.**
- Hire someone with a **new composite of experiences and skills.**

The process used to select new people (whether staff, independent contractor or vendor) demonstrates your organization's culture. Remember, culture is about behaviors, not slogans. Your selection process is the initial confirmation that your organization's culture is one that values leadership thinking.

Selection Process for a Culture of Valued Leadership

► **Consult** *with current associates to:*

- Explore the bigger picture opportunities.
- Gain clarity of duties of the new associate.
- Validate their leadership responsibilities.

> *"It is not just about what we are currently doing.*
> *It is about where we are heading."*

► **Identify** *desired outcomes.*

- Move beyond the 'stuff' that has to get done.

> *"Does the 'stuff' we will do move us toward desired*
> *outcomes or just more 'stuff?'"*

► **Select** *requisites for eligibility.*

- Identify skills, knowledge, and experience.

> *"Are there valid reasons to include each requisite?"*

► **Utilize** *experienced-based questions. (These questions focus on how the candidate actually handled past interactions, assignments, etc.)*

- Generate specifics not generalities.

> *"Does the candidate possess relevant skills?*
> *Will their methods and style fit the organization?"*

► **Make** *a jointly (candidate and organization) agreed upon, quality business decision.*

> *"The organization wants people who want the organization."*

The Fog of Competency

An eligible candidate satisfies a list of qualifications. These usually include education, professional credentials, knowledge, and skills. Determining eligibility is relatively easy.

Determining that a candidate is a match for the specific position is not easy. Why? The candidate's knowledge, skills, and competency are wrapped within their own unique package of style, interests, and professional beliefs.

The issue of competency is an interesting ingredient of selection. In Chapter 4 we explored the challenge of labels. The word competency is a label used to describe a significant level of capability and effectiveness. As with most labels, this one does not add clarity. We often hear such statements as, *"Dick has the competency to handle the job,"* or *"Jane is (is not) demonstrating the competency to be an effective . . . school principal . . . union leader . . . band director . . . supervisor of widgets . . . senior vice president of whatever . . . CEO."*

The label of competency tends to be used in a global context. That is, the person either is or is not. When we acknowledge that an individual's current level of professional capability is comprised of multiple competencies, we increase our capacity to match people to opportunities. We also increase our capacity to coach.

Although the foundation of competency is knowledge and skills, competency encompasses a broader context. Competencies are developed over time. People can progress, or not, from basic levels to advanced levels. Basic levels are about understanding and effectively engaging the rudimental elements. Higher levels require the ability to coach others in that competency area. Advanced levels are demonstrated by creating newness of thought and impact.

It is normal for people to be able to perform at higher levels for some elements of a competency and lower or minimal levels with other elements. It is unrealistic to expect otherwise.

Let's look at an example. Assume you have the opportunity to hire someone to lead a team of experienced people. You interview a candidate. During the interview you say, *"Tell me about your most recent* *leadership role and how you would assess your level of leadership skills."* The candidate provides details and confidently states she has a high level of leadership competency. You think to yourself, *"Awesome, that is just what we need, a confident leader. And since I loathe interviewing candidates, I will just congratulate myself on my amazing ability to select new people and offer her the job."*

Perhaps we can enhance this approach. Since this position requires leadership capabilities, let's take a look at leadership competency. If you were to create a list of components that contribute to leadership competency, what would be included in your list? Take a minute. Ponder what items would make your list.

Now examine the following list of components that contribute to leadership competency.

- Self-Leadership
- Conceptual and Entrepreneurial Thinking
- Defining Purpose—Answering the Why Questions
- People Development
- Executive Effectiveness
- Establishing Expectations and Accountability
- Ability to Listen
- Openness to Innovation

Are there any matches to your list? Which items, if any, would be important for a candidate to be successful in a specific position in your organization? How would you access the level of competency required for each item you deem significant to that position?

The above list is not meant to be "the list" but it does acknowledge that a competency is comprised of multiple components. That recognition enables us to assess our job openings as well as our candidates with more clarity.

One item on the above list, executive effectiveness, is a topic addressed by Peter Drucker in his book, *The Effective Executive*.[3] If you have not read this book multiple times, I encourage you to do so.

Selection Competency

Leadership competency includes the ability to identify components of a competency relevant to an open position. Once those components are identified, you can use experience-based questions that reference key elements of your organization's culture into your selection process. The resulting dialogue will assist both the candidate and the selection team to make a jointly agreed upon, quality business decision as to whether the position and the candidate are a good match.

Here are some examples of how elements of an organization's culture can be integrated into the dialogue of interviewing a candidate:

- *Advancing our personal professional knowledge and skills is important to our organization's continuing success. Tell me how you identified an area of professional growth you wanted to enhance. How did you pursue that additional knowledge and skill? How did you engage that knowledge and skill in your activities?*

- *Our professional activities create opportunities to observe, listen, and learn. Tell me about an insight you gained in the last year and how you are engaging that insight in your leadership practices.*

- *Our associates take pride in identifying and being accountable for outcomes. Tell me about how you determined specific outcomes for a project and then established accountability for those outcomes.*

- *Efficiency is important to our organization. So is effectiveness. Share with me an example of how you have increased your personal effectiveness recently.*

---

2 *The Effective Executive*, Peter F. Drucker, Copyright 1967, HarperCollins Publishers. ISBN 0-06-051607-0

- *Knowing the "whys" empowers people. What is a "why" question you have been asked recently and what was your answer? What is a "why" question you have for us?*

Each of the above combinations of information and question gives the candidate important insight about your organization. Each facilitates inquiry from both the candidate and the selection team.

How could you tailor each of the above examples to make them relevant to your organization? What follow-up questions would you use to determine whether the candidate and your organization can be a good match?

Perhaps you feel it is unrealistic to expect leaders to allocate the time to pursue this level of candidate inquiry. Your preference may be a "Let's just get someone hired and let them figure things out" approach. I admit a solid argument can be made for that type of approach, especially in an environment of high volume hiring.

What I am campaigning for, however, is a selection process that is evidence your organization's culture seeks new associates in a context of opportunity.

As stated earlier, the **opportunity** of adding a new associate is not about just determining if the candidate can do the job. The opportunity is about whether **the person can engage their unique composite of knowledge, skills, and competencies** in the specific situation to generate quality outcomes. The opportunity is about creating **synergy within the ensemble of talent** in the organization. The opportunity is about **openness to possibilities** and progressing to something better.

Competency- My Perspective

- Competency is comprised of multiple components.

- Individuals possess advanced levels in some areas—lesser or minimal in others.

- Competency is created over time.

- Advanced competency welcomes newness of knowledge, skills, ideas, and insights.

- A significant **element of competency** enabling individuals to contribute unique value to their organization **results from their experience within the organization**.

So do we pretend to hire, as well as assign, new responsibilities only to people with advanced levels of competency? Or do we expand our options by identifying people who are at a *readiness level* to accept these opportunities? I vote for door number two. My experience says selection based on readiness is both a reality and a benefit to organizations.

If we wait for someone to be fully competent, whatever that means, versus being at a level of readiness to assume new responsibilities, we will be contributing to a culture of valued fiction, not a culture of valued leadership.

In cultures of valued leadership individuals embrace the concept that they are the **leader of their professional development**. Primed with this belief, each person can identify opportunities to expand their professionalism.

In the next chapter we will explore how organizations can utilize "Readiness Paths" to develop talent and reinforce the mindset of continuous professional development.

"Competency embraces listening and learning.

Chapter 11

Readiness

"Once we grasp that we get to be the leader of our professional development, we progress on our path of readiness. By promoting readiness, organizations attract and retain great talent."

Organizations would love to have all new associates immediately know it all and be able to do it all. Some new associates pretend they do and can. They likely also fantasize about being a super hero. The wiser ones understand that competency is acquired over time. And they know the component of their competency that enables them to contribute significant value to their organization results from their experience within that organization.

Organizations can choose to just throw people into the performance pool to see if sinking or swimming results. Many entrepreneurs brag that they jumped in and then learned to swim. Some swam. We mourn the ones who did not. Or at least we mourn our investment dollars that sank with them. The more insightful entrepreneurs enhance their readiness before jumping.

I advocate for a development approach based on these two ideas:

- Every associate **"gets to"** bring leadership to their personal professional development.
- Every organization **"gets to"** bring leadership to the development of their associates.

People joining or moving to a new area of responsibility in an organization appreciate and benefit from "readiness" support. Such support might include training manuals, courses, workshops, job shadowing, coaching, and mentoring. I advocate enhancing this package by including a sequence of learning activities, which I call "Readiness Paths."

Readiness paths enable participants to:

- Determine their level of interest and match for the opportunity.
- Understand the duties and responsibilities.
- Know the requirements for eligibility.
- Build layers of knowledge and skills.
- Progress to incremental levels of professional engagement.

Readiness Paths enable the organization to:

- Reinforce a mindset of continuous professional growth.
- Create students of the organization and its competitive environment.
- Promote opportunity thinking.
- Engage people's natural talents and interests.
- Reward professionalism.
- Deliver valued leadership.

Readiness paths can be used in many situations:

- New career evaluation and preparation.
- Orientation/screening for people exploring new opportunities.
- Career launch and development.
- Create pipeline of candidates.
- Development of specialists.
- Not-for-profit—volunteer development.

Here are two scenarios where readiness paths can be a valuable resource.

- A business with multiple offices; each office has a director of operations. These people are frequently promoted into new roles. The organization will benefit from being able to select from a pool of candidates "ready" to quickly fill these vacancies.
- A not-for-profit organization has multiple opportunities for volunteers. These volunteers can choose to progress to expanded levels of responsibilities, knowledge, and skills. The organization wants to create a flow of people "ready" to step in.

Readiness paths of learning activities are based on the lessons gathered from people who are in, or have tried to be in, the jobs for which the path is targeted. If resources were unlimited, customized paths could be created for each person. Since that is unrealistic, the readiness paths are designed so they can be utilized by multiple people. And since these folks will be at different levels of knowledge and skills, each person can progress at a different pace. Each experience on the path enables participants to explore their interests while expanding their knowledge, skills, and insights.

Any organization that employs multiple people in comparable roles, (i.e., managers of offices/retail outlets/franchises, supervisors of business units, advanced knowledge associates, etc.), can benefit from engaging readiness paths.

A Model Readiness Path

A readiness path is a sequence of targeted learning experiences. Each experience enables participants to explore their level of interest and fit for the role while expanding their capabilities.

I recommend that readiness paths include these components:

► **Desired Outcomes:**

- For the organization.
- For the participants.

► **Assumptions/Realities:**

- Things we acknowledge/things we do not pretend do not exist.

► **Guidelines/Practice Standards:**

- Philosophy of approach.
- Expectations/Accountability.
- Disclosures—no "hidden" agendas—includes "regulatory/ mandatory" issues.

► **Phases/Modules:**

- Complete one; progress to next.
- Each includes objectives, learning experiences, timelines.

► **Upon completion, the participants will have acquired/ accomplished:**

- Specific items that demonstrate progress.

▶ **Upon completion, the organization will have acquired/ accomplished:**

- Specific items that demonstrate progress for the organization.

▶ **Facilitator Support Resources:**

- Assumptions and expectations.
- Strategies, standards, style.

Here are examples of items that might appear under each of the above components:

▶ **Desired outcomes:**

- **For organization:**
    - *Enhanced understanding of competitive variables.*
    - *Increased self-leadership.*
    - *Pool of eligible candidates.*
    - *Knowledge and skill gaps identified.*
    - *"Ah-ha's" (i.e. 'Now, we understand why...").*
    - *Informed career decisions.*
- **For participants:**
    - *Expectations are understood.*
    - *Knowledge and skill gaps identified.*
    - *Professional beliefs are acknowledged.*
    - *"Why", "What-if" and "Would it be possible" questions answered.*
    - *"Ah-ha's" (i.e. "Now, I understand...").*
    - *Informed career decision.*

► **Assumptions/ Realities:**

- Participants are expected to take ownership of preparation.
- Focus is on demonstrating, observing, confirming candidates 'can do'.

► **Guidelines/Practice Standards:**

- Foundational knowledge and skills required prior to "path" participation.
- Verbal "information dumps" to be avoided—reference resources to be utilized.
- Realistic case studies are major component of learning.
- "Stories" of obstacles/challenges to overcome are shared.
- Clarity of what defines success.

► **Phases/Modules—each includes:**

- Objectives.
- Learning experiences.
- Expectations.
- Accountability.

► **Upon completion, participants will have:**

- Validated their level of interest to pursue new opportunity.
- Obtained necessary requisites (certifications, licenses, etc.).
- Completed six month business plan.
- Demonstrated specific skills.
- Validated opportunity matches professional interests.
- Decision to continue on the path or not.

▶ **Upon completion, the organization (facilitators/selection team) will have:**

- Validated required level of knowledge and skills.
- Identified next level knowledge/skills to be acquired.

▶ **Facilitator Support Resources:**

- Assignment guides.
- Dialogue questions.
- Situations to resolve.

Apply the Model to Your Organization

Let's see how this model can apply to your organization. Refer to the readiness path examples shown earlier. Identify a comparable opportunity in your organization. Now, using the above examples as a guide, write down potential components for that readiness path in your organization:

▶ **Desired Outcomes:**

- For the organization:

  ○ _____

  ○ _____

- For the participants:

  ○ _____

  ○ _____

▶ **Assumptions/Realities:**

  ○ _____

  ○ _____

▶ **Guidelines/Practice Standards:**

    ○ _____

    ○ _____

▶ **Phases/Modules***:*

    ○ _____

    ○ _____

    ○ _____

    ○ _____

▶ **Upon completion, the participants will have***:*

    ○ _____

    ○ _____

    ○ _____

    ○ _____

▶ **Upon completion, the organization will have***:*

   ○ _____

   ○ _____

   ○ _____

   ○ _____

▶ **Facilitator Support Resources:**

   ○ _____

   ○ _____

   ○ _____

   ○ _____

How is a Readiness Path Created?

> *Standardized versus Customized . . . Uniformity versus*
> *Flexibility . . . Event versus Process . . . Latitude versus One*
> *Size Fits All . . . Definition versus Lack of Definition . . .*
> *Just tell me versus Let me figure it out . . . Structure versus*
> *Randomness?*

Substance and style ingredients of tactics aimed at advancing people's individual professional development are limitless. That reality creates opportunities. Creating readiness paths helps organizations capture those opportunities. The process begins with questions.

The first question is: *"What are our **desired outcomes?** "*

It will be a natural reaction to answer this question with operational metrics, i.e., improvements in sales, margins, expenses, units of distribution, net profits, etc. Readiness paths, however, focus on a broader perspective. Here are a few examples:

- Sustainable pipeline of eligible candidates.
- Culture where only prepared people are promoted.
- Sustainable system of leadership development.
- Diversity of talent collaborating on next generation opportunities.
- Community of talent committed to mentoring others.

Grab a piece of paper or your trusty mobile device. Quickly, record a few desired outcomes you have for your area of influence. Do not stress over perfect wording. Just capture a few ideas. These initial thoughts will be your catalyst to clarify your desired outcomes. That clarity will become the foundation of your readiness path. The readiness path will become the foundation of your organizational development efforts.

Next, ponder the likely desired outcomes you might hear expressed by your peers. By anticipating their potential responses, you will be prepared to coach.

Then, use questions such as these to dig deeper:

- **Q–** What is our unique value proposition?

- **Q–** Why us (versus our competitors)?

- **Q–** What are currently our big opportunities? Significant obstacles?

- **Q–** What are the professional beliefs we see being used by our associates? Are they valid?

- **Q**– What is the model client experience we want to create?

- **Q**– To what degree do we need to validate levels of knowledge and or skills? (For example, regulatory requirements may need to be satisfied, etc.)

- **Q**– How will effectiveness be determined?

Note: None of these questions address operational metrics. By omitting such questions, I am not implying that scoreboard metrics are not relevant. I am suggesting that readiness paths are focused on expanding capabilities to take the organization to new places. Understanding the 'why's' of scoreboard metrics will be important elements for our readiness path activities. The ability to generate improved metrics will result from expanding the capabilities of your team of associates.

With your desired outcomes identified, you and your team will benefit from initiating a fresh look at the responsibilities and activities for which the readiness path is targeted. Here are a few things to address:

- What do people in these positions actually do?
- What resources do they utilize?
- What knowledge, skills, and understanding enable them to excel?
- What obstructs their effectiveness?
- What suggestions are they offering?

It is amazing how quickly roles, practices, knowledge, skills, and resources change. Without a fresh examination of these variables, your readiness path will become irrelevant. With a fresh examination, your readiness path of "practicum" experiences will continue to add value.

The term "practicum" reminds us to be practical and realistic. To assure clarity here are a few examples of practicum exercises:

- Prospective client conversations: introduction, discovery, solution presentations
- Day in the Life: activities and metrics
- Competitive products analysis

Each practicum experience placed on the path has a specific purpose. Collectively, they target the desired outcomes.

Is This Too Complicated to be Realistic?

About now you may be throwing up your hands saying this is more complex than I or my organization has the capacity to support. Let me pull you back from this emotional *"Are you kidding me...Don't you know how overwhelmed I am?"* ledge before you lose your balance. Don't get overly caught up in the details. Get caught up in the concept.

If creating a readiness path seems too challenging, just add a "readiness component" as a preamble to an existing process or program. This addition can enhance your organization's ability to match opportunities to people's interest and talent. It can reduce the energy and dollars spent training people who are not matched or ready to pursue the opportunities.

Readiness paths enable people to explore opportunities of professionalism. Those opportunities may take the form of progressing up the ladder of the organization's hierarchy. They may move people to the next level of skill, knowledge, and competency. They may be focused on encouraging and facilitating enhanced collaboration. Regardless, the paths aim to expand the participant's and the organization's capabilities.

In organizations **where leadership is valued**, associates are encouraged to continuously advance their readiness levels. In these organizations, coaching, mentoring, and readiness mindsets are evident.

I do not understand why people would allow their professional time to be consumed by organizations that do not exhibit these practices and this mindset.

> *"Although readiness paths may include benches along the way where people can reflect and pontificate upon their expanding talent set, the benches are only resting spots. The paths continue."*

My professional beliefs that lead me to promote the use of readiness paths:

- *People want to enhance their professional capability.*
- *People can be and want to be the leader of their personal professional development.*
- *Organizational vitality relies on the professional development of its associates.*
- *Organizations enhance their attractiveness to current and potential associates through proactive professional development programs.*

Chapter 12

Next Steps

I believe every associate can be the leader of her or his professional development. As leaders, we can express advocacy for this idea by posing this simple question, "What do you see as the next step along your path of professional development?"

This question creates opportunities to listen, learn, teach, and coach. It encourages every person to be on a continuous path of professional development. And it acknowledges and respects each individual.

Let's make this personal. Ask yourself, *"What is the next step in my professional development?"* If you have a specific answer, pick a specific date to take that next step. If not, open your calendar. Find two one-hour time slots, two or three days apart, during the portion of your day when you do your best thinking. Schedule an appointment for each time slot. Title the appointment, **"Next Step."** Now, move one week ahead in your calendar. Find another available hour during your prime productive time. Again, enter your **"Next Step"** appointment. Now, schedule a **"Next Step"** appointment each week for the next six weeks.

Nice job. You have created a meaningful and doable commitment to your professional development.

Preparing for your "Next Step" Appointments

Now, create a **"Next Step" Journal** to record your notes and track your actions. Use your electronic toy of choice or a pad of paper. The tool makes no difference. Having a journal does make a difference.

Add a **"Things to Ponder"** section in your journal with these categories:

- *Professional Beliefs (ones I want to tout, ones I want to replace)*
- *Things that got in my way today*
- *Topics I would like to ask about/ explore*
- *Knowledge that would have been helpful to me today*
- *Skills that would have been useful to me today*
- *If I could, I would...*

Keep your journal easily accessible to remind you to capture your thoughts as they occur.

Here are some **"Next Step" Questions** to add to your journal:

- **Q**–What **skill(s)** do I want to add/enhance?

    - **Why?** *What will be the specific* **benefits** *to me/my team/my organization?*
- **Q**– What **knowledge** do I want to gain concerning: Our organization? Competitive environment? My "turf" within the organization?

    - **Why?** *What will be the specific* **benefits** *to me/my team/my organization?*
- **Q**– What specific **area of interest** do I want **to investigate/ research**?

    - **Why?** *What will be the specific* **benefits** *to me/my team/my organization?*

- What **information/question** do I want to explore with my peers/organization?

  - **Why?** *What will be the specific* **benefits** *to me/my team/my organization?*

- What is getting in the way of my professional development?

  - **Why?** *What will be the specific benefits to me of removing this interference?*

- **Q–** Which of my **professional beliefs** need to be replaced?

  - **Why?** *What will be the specific* **benefits** *to me/my team/my organization?*

- **Q–** Which of my **professional beliefs** are proving beneficial/creating better outcomes?

  - **Why?** *What will be the specific* **benefits** *to me/my team/my organization if I continue to act on these beliefs?*

- **Q– Who** could I invite to be an **accountability partner**?

  - **What do I want** *from this relationship?*

- **Q– Who** could I invite to be a **mentor?**

  - **What do I want** *from this relationship?*

The possibilities for **"Next Steps"** are limitless. Remember, **"Next Steps"** are not about right or wrong. They are about being proactive in your thinking and your actions.

Your First "My Next Step" Appointment

When your appointment time arrives you will be tempted to postpone it. After all, you are important, overwhelmed, and far too busy to be bothered with personal growth stuff. Resist this temptation. You resisted the temptation to stay in bed this morning. You resisted a sixth cup of coffee today. You can handle this. Go ahead and arrive on time for your appointment.

Start your appointment by reviewing the notes you have made in your journal. As you reflect on those notes, jot down any new ideas that arise. Don't critique them. Just consider them gifts.

You will find you are more focused on some items than others. Concentrate on those items. Repeat the **"Next Step"** questions with focus on those topics.

Identify a next step that is immediately doable. For example, your next step cannot be "Obtain an MBA." Your next step, however, can, be to research the MBA degree program options available in your area.

As you approach the end of your appointment, write down your **"Next Step."** The act of writing or hitting the keyboard brings clarity to what you are going to do.

There is always a **"Next Step"** to take on your path of professional development. Be proud that you are the leader who defines your **"Next Step."**

By placing this initial series of **"Next Step"** appointments on your calendar, you have created a mindset that enables you to continue down your path of professional development. Enjoy your journey.

Promoting "Next Steps" Thinking In Your Organizations

If you are in a leadership role for others, officially or unofficially, you can promote **"Next Step"** thinking and practices for their benefit. Here are ways to do so.

Share Your Story

Personal stories are powerful. Sharing why you initiated your **"Next Step"** process, and why you selected the step you are now completing, demonstrates realness. It also makes you vulnerable to being critiqued and held accountable. Move ahead anyway. People will be interested in what you are learning and why it is of interest to you. They will be interested in the next **"Next Step"** you select. They will be interested in why you made that choice.

Your willingness to share your experiences will encourage others to identify a **"Next Step"** in their professional development.

Integrate "Next Step" Into Your One-on-One Coaching

If you have responsibility for other associates, you are likely engaged in a regular flow of one-on-one interactions. Demonstrate valued leadership by integrating a **"Next Step"** component into these interactions. You can introduce the process by sharing how you utilize **"Next Step"** thinking in your professional development efforts. Trust is the required ingredient for success. Trust evolves from consistency of experience.

By the way, consider the opportunities for **"Next Step"** thinking and activities in the lives of others within your sphere of influence. Think children, grandchildren, nieces and nephews. Remember, sharing your story influences receptivity.

Integrate "Next Steps" Into your Work Teams

Project teams are always taking steps to achieve their goals. And, yes, sometimes those steps are lateral or backwards. Expect it. Then use the **"Next Step"** conversation to refocus the group. The simplicity of the idea helps cut through the complexity of the interactions. If the group is getting consumed by the expression of multiple viewpoints, you can be a positive influence by posing these questions:

- **Q–** *What are our desired outcomes?*

- **Q–** *How will we know they have been achieved?*

- **Q–** *What is the "Next Step" we can take that will benefit our efforts?*

Note: Since this is a group effort, multiple **"Next Steps"** can likely be taken by different individuals. By identifying a leader and a timetable for each next step, incremental valued leadership can surface.

Remember, Advocacy is Powerful

"Next Step" thinking and action is about advocacy. So be an advocate for yourself and others.

*"By adding **"Next Step"** thinking to your professional practices and **"Next Step"** appointments to your calendar, you are creating an invigorating pattern for self-improvement. You are delivering **valued leadership**."*

Chapter 13

Desired Outcomes

I like the term **"Desired Outcomes"** because it cuts through the distractions of goals, objectives, strategies, and tactics jargon. I define this term as **"significance to be achieved."** When we seek to define our desired outcomes, the focus is on our purpose rather than on our busyness. Once desired outcomes are defined, appropriate tactics can be selected.

Let me share a couple of scenarios that illustrate this concept.

Scenario 1

Assume you are a member of a not-for-profit board. The board decides to add a music festival to its calendar of events. Because you were an advocate for the festival idea (and you did not exit the meeting room fast enough), you are now the chairperson of the festival committee. Now what? How do you, in addition to being an effective task master for this project, add value?

You arrive for your committee's first meeting. While preparing to start the meeting, you hear people sharing lots of "need-to" and "got-to" comments spliced into an abundance of "What if we did . . . We could . . . Why don't we try . . . ." suggestions. You also hear strong opinions expressed about single- or multi-day formats, multiple stages, food and merchandise vendors, special viewing areas for donors, and whether the mayor should speak.

So how do you immediately deliver value?

You ask, **"What opportunities to advance our mission and progress toward our vision can we capture through this event?"** Or simply ask, **"What are our desired outcomes?"** These questions move people from details to outcomes. The answers to these questions become the foundation for resource decisions. The group dynamic created by asking and answering these questions **validates a culture of valued leadership.**

Scenario 2

Assume you are placed on a team of your peers. The team's assignment is to deliver a training conference for a large group of your organization's managers. Assume the team has been given the always popular, *"We want to make these people better"* mission statement.

The team calls its initial meeting. Someone starts the discussion by asking, *"What are we going to do with these people when they get here next month . . . next week . . . tomorrow?"* Team members quickly chime in with an abundance of *"We should . . . we could"* suggestions. Then, after much bantering, a frustrated soul says, *"Let's just pick some of these and get on with it."*

Bolstered by this "take charge, please get this over with suggestion," participants begin a frenzied debate about the sequence and length of time each subject matter expert should use to share their abundant knowledge. Magically, a flow of presentations (more stuff than anyone can possibly absorb) is turned into an agenda. Although I love magic, let me offer an alternative to this frequently viewed reality show.

Instead of beginning by asking, *"What are we going to do with these people?"* begin by asking, **"What are our desired outcomes for our managers and for our organization?"**

Don't be surprised if the immediate reactions to your question are blank stares. Don't panic. Reflection is good for the soul. Give it a few seconds. If the blank stares continue, pose a few of the following questions:

- **Q–** *We are going to spend a significant amount of our professional time, energy, and organizational dollars on this event. What do we want to accomplish?*

- **Q–** *What potential beneficial outcomes are we overlooking?*

- **Q–** *Let's assume the event is over. A few weeks have passed. We feel good about the event. What would make that true? What has been, and is being, impacted?*

- **Q–** *What are the desired outcomes for our less experienced participants? For our more experienced participants?*

- **Q–** *What if we are asked to make a presentation to senior management on the results of this event? What observations would we share? What would we brag about? What will we say has or will improve based on our efforts? What will we say we learned? What "next steps" will we recommend to enhance the results of our investment?*

- **Q–** *What will be useful information to enable us to evaluate whether this event was a good investment of time, talent, and organization dollars?*

Rarely does a team have the luxury of conducting a strategic planning process prior to executing assignments. Always, however, the team has the opportunity to enhance its effectiveness by exploring the ***"What are our desired outcomes"*** question. Once the desired outcomes are scrutinized and clarified, the "What to do" and "Whether to do" decisions become easier.

The group can make yes/no decisions on the normal flow of "We could . . . Why don't we . . . What if we" ideas by **answering these two simple questions**:

- **Q**– Will it contribute to our "Desired Outcomes"?

- **Q**– Do we have the capacity to effectively execute this idea at this time?

What if, in place of the above approach, this team had started their process by asking, *"What are our goals and objectives?"* The responses would likely have sounded like the following: *"To have 25–30 people qualify to attend"; "Stay within our budget"; "Seven and one-half hours of continuing education credits"; "Make sure we allocate time for the CEO to pontificate."*

Granted, these responses may be relevant, but where is the greater purpose? What is the impact? Is our goal merely to stay within budget boundaries and have every participant receive seven and one-half hours of continuing education credits? Or are our desired outcomes about new capabilities, strengthened professional beliefs, and enhanced professional pride? Asking about goals and objectives makes it too easy to get caught up in metrics that may have little to do with significance.

Desired Outcomes- Then Goals and Objectives. Let's Get Specific.

By focusing first on mission/vision-driven desired outcomes, we promote opportunity thinking. Once our desired outcomes are identified, supportive goals and objectives can be defined.

Here are examples of desired outcomes with supportive goals and objectives. Note how the desired outcomes open a range of possibilities of goals, strategies, and tactics. Note the broader context of the desired outcome versus the tighter focus of the goals and objectives.

▶ **Professional Development Conference:**

- ***Desired Outcome:*** *New associates own the professional belief that they can deliver unique value to their specific markets.*

- Related Goals and Objectives:
    - ○ *Proprietary client assessment tools effectively utilized by all associates.*
    - ○ *20 percent average increase in business volume at end of following three months.*

▶ **Arts Organization Annual Event:**

- ***Desired Outcome:*** *Organization owns a unique identity in the national landscape.*

- ***Desired Outcome:*** *Enhanced reputation and respect for arts educators.*

- ***Related Goals and Objectives:***
    - ○ *Event attendance increases 25 percent each year for following three years.*
    - ○ *$50,000 net revenue for underwriting future education programs.*
    - ○ *National/international attendees represent 15 percent of the audience.*

▶ **Parent-Teacher Organization:**

- ***Desired Outcome:*** *Parents and teachers are active advocates for school's mission, vision, and practices.*

- ***Desired Outcome:*** *Parents and teachers are a community of support for students.*

- ***Related Goals and Objectives:***
    - ○ *35 percent of operations costs are covered through fund-raising activities.*
    - ○ *Fundraising efforts generate 15 percent increase over current year.*
    - ○ *Three new members are added to the faculty.*

► **Youth Sports Organization***:*

- ***Desired Outcome****: Parents, coaches, and referees are advocates for respectful competitiveness.*

- ***Desired Outcome:*** *All participants advance their knowledge, skills, and respect for the sport and sportsmanship.*

- ***Desired Outcome:*** *Sustainable funding.*

- ***Related Goals and Objectives****:*
  - *Player skills and sportsmanship clinics offered— target of 85 percent participation.*
  - *Increase number of teams by 20 percent over next two years.*
  - *Increase number of coaches by 20 percent over the next two years.*
  - *Number of referee clinics increased by 50 percent.*

Now, using the above examples as a guide, use the following space to define desired outcomes and related goals for your organizations. Remember, desired outcomes are items you consider to be of significance to the organization. For each desired outcome, identify specific goals and objectives that will contribute to these desired outcomes.

Where you work: _____

- ***Desired Outcome(s):*** _____

_____

_____

- ***Related Goals and Objectives*:** _____

  _____

  _____

Where you volunteer your time:_____

- ***Desired Outcome(s)*:** _____

  _____

  _____

- ***Related Goals and Objectives*:** _____

  _____

  _____

Here's the thing. Desired outcomes are the tangibles of mission and vision. Our openness to explore and then select meaningful outcomes both **scrutinizes and advances our organization's mission and vision**. Our openness to ponder alternatives **expands our grasp of our organization's purpose and its opportunities**. The discipline of defining desired outcomes **delivers valued leadership**.

A Final Thought

Desired outcomes always face obstacles. Obstacles are often in the form of "lacks," i.e., lack of funding . . . understanding . . . personnel . . . participation . . . entrepreneurial spirit . . . passion . . . . . . solutions . . . community support . . . vision.

Obstacles, or problems as we like to label them, can be simple or complex. Regardless of complexity, when obstacles are viewed in a context of desired outcomes, they can become an amazing catalyst for creative and opportunity-focused thinking. That thinking can lead to innovative next steps.

Chapter 14

First, Define the Whats and Whys

Like the term "desired outcomes," these three little words, **Whats, Whys,** and **Hows,** also can cut through organizational jargon. Valued leadership insists that "Whats" and "Whys" are defined before "Hows" are addressed.

By **"Whats"** I mean things we want to accomplish. I also mean the activities where we will allow energy, intellectual property, and resources to be utilized.

By **"Whys"** I mean the reasons and the benefits of the **"Whats."** Valued leadership demands **"Whys."** (*"We could not think of a better thing to do"* and *"Why don't we just give this a try?"* do not qualify as "Whys.")

By **"Hows"** I mean the details of getting stuff done.

My observation is that folks will readily jump into discussions about "Hows" before, if ever, defining "Whats" and "Whys"? And why is that? The "Hows" are easier. Everyone has ideas and opinions they are willing to share about how to do stuff. So they do.

You are familiar with the "How" conversations. You have participated in them many times. They start when someone says, *"What if . . . I have always wondered why we haven't tried . . . I think we should sell raffle tickets . . . My brother-in-law can help us."* These interactions become feeding frenzies of *"We could... We should... What if the event started at 4 p.m. instead of 5 p.m."* ideas.

These dynamics continue because the busyness of throwing out ideas feels productive. Usually no one captures these ideas unless an inspired participant, armed with a pungent smelling erasable pen, dashes to the white board, or someone opens a mind map app on their PC to create a tapestry of organizational idea art. And what is the final element of this dynamic? Participants exit the gathering without anyone owning any next moves.

Although these idea-sharing exchanges are not easy to productively redirect, I have confidence we can do so. And we can do so in a manner that does not diminish the enthusiasm of the people in the group. Here's how.

First, **"Break the Flow"** of the "hows" before the "whats" and "whys" conversations. You can do that by saying:

> *"We are offering lots of ideas that can enhance our ability to execute our event and we have an opportunity to accomplish some very positive outcomes. So that I can offer good input, I want to make sure I understand what we hope to accomplish. I think one of the outcomes we want is _____. Is that accurate? What other desired outcomes do we want?"*

Or, you can take a more blunt approach and say:

> *"Come on people. We are throwing out all kinds of ideas on how we can do stuff but we haven't agreed on what we want to accomplish and why. We need to get it together."*

Recall the most recent how-to idea-generating exchange you experienced. Ask yourself:

- **Q–** How did the "What if we . . ." sharing commence?

- **Q–** How did it conclude? Did anyone exit with **"Next Steps"** assignments?

- **Q–** When did an opportunity appear to assist the group to define the "whys"?

- **Q–** Given the mix of participants and the level of importance of the task being discussed, what **"Break the Flow"** comment could you have contributed?

Assuring Clarity

Frequently the "Whats" are described with nice sounding phrases like: "improved sales," "enhanced skills," "improved communication," or the ever popular "Get people to think outside the box." Who could argue with these? They sound worthwhile.

They are also vague, impossible to measure, and a potential match for any *"We could do this . . . We could try that . . ."* tactic. You can use some of the following questions to help the group progress to a *"So what we really want to accomplish is . . ."* level of clarity:

- **Q-** *Does this effort contribute to advancing our mission and vision?*

- **Q-** *Does this project/event/study justify our collective efforts?*

- **Q-** *Let's pretend we completed our project/event/study program. What will be the benefits to our organization?* To help participants identify specific benefits, ask about benefits to the various stakeholder groups. Examples:

  - *Departments, divisions, senior management, board of directors*
  - *New associates, experienced associates*
  - *Clients, patrons*
  - *Specialists—product, marketing, information technology, human resources*
  - *Vendor partners, business community, city and civic leaders*
  - *The industry in which the organization resides*

- **Q-** *Would our outcomes generate excitement from each group of stakeholders?*
  - **Q-** *Would our peers wish they had been able to participate?*
  - **Q-** *Would our outcomes generate new investments or contributions?*

- **Q-** *What opportunities do we have now to create interest in our efforts? What could our "pre-story" include?*

- **Q-** *Given the outcomes we are targeting, are we selecting the strategy and tactics that match our desired outcomes?*

- **Q-** *As we are congratulating ourselves on our success, what might we be saying we could have **also** achieved if we had only thought of it earlier?*

- **Q-** *We are writing the communications about our success. What's the **headline**?*

- **Q-** *Will these tactics, even if executed effectively, achieve our desired outcomes?*

- **Q-** How will we answer when someone asks, "So what?"

- **Q-** *Seriously, what are we trying to accomplish?*

These questions can generate opportunity thinking and informed collaboration. In cultures of valued leadership, all stakeholders are encouraged to be curious, to be students of the organization. Their curiosity leads to greater clarity. That clarity leads to improved results.

Chapter 15

Metrics

An organizational equivalent of a ceremonial dance is the hoopla surrounding announcements that, *"We hit our numbers for the week . . . quarter . . . year"* or *"We exceeded Wall Street's quarterly earnings expectations."* Even if cake and ice cream are served, the ceremony and the dance are soon forgotten.

When metrics dominate organizational conversations, purpose becomes background noise and opportunities are missed. Purpose, not metrics, inspires people to deliver valued leadership.

Yes, metrics inform. They provide numerical perspective about success or non-success. They can enable stakeholders to be students of the organization. They can be a source of organizational discipline. They can also be a source of distraction. They are rarely a source of inspiration.

> *People do not get up in the morning and say, "I want to improve my metrics today."*

Let's role-play a metrics-focused presentation. It goes something like this. A three-piece suit says, *"As you can see from this first graphic, our sales increased by 5 percent and our profit margin advanced from*

21.5–22 percent. We are moving in the right direction. I hope you are proud that your efforts are moving our numbers. Based on the trend line over the past few periods, we should soon be able to hit our targets of 6.5 percent and 24.5 percent. Then we can really be proud. Any questions?"

A brave but likely-to-be-departing-soon soul says, *"Yes, I have a question. Why will we be proud that we hit some arbitrary percentages?"* A hush comes over the room as the three-piece suit responds, *"Because those are the numbers I promised our majority stockholder, my father-in-law, we would hit."* The soon-to-be departing associate shrugs. The three-piece suit, given his concise response, assumes the audience is thinking, *"Wow, that was awesome. We have never had that question answered so clearly. We are inspired by our leader and we cannot wait to hear what is announced for next year's target percentages."*

Is this role play exaggerated? Yes, but only because it included the "arbitrary percentages" question. Reflect on the many times you sat through presentations about your organization's metrics. How long did it take you to forget the data and just get back to your daily activities?

Let's consider an alternative presentation.

The head honcho says, *"Thanks for carving out some time on your schedules to be here this morning. I promise we will be respectful of your time. We are going to focus on our business analytics. To start, we are going to hear from three of our associates. Each of them has a story to share about a recent interaction they had in our marketplace. Once they finish they will answer any questions and invite you to share your observations. I think their experiences will help us evaluate our financial results."*

After the three associates share their experiences, the head honcho continues,

"As you just heard, the first two experiences related to existing clients who are benefitting from the new level of value we are able to deliver because of the collective efforts of all of you. The last experience is an example of a significant market need we are not currently able to meet. It may become an opportunity for us to pursue in the future. When I first heard about these market interactions, I asked several questions to make sure I understood the situations. What questions do you have

for our presenters? What observations do you have concerning client experiences you have had recently?"

The head honcho now continues, *"Our organization's mission is _____. Our vision is _____. All of us value curiosity, innovation, and effectiveness. We also value structuring our business practices to include time to listen and learn from our clients and our not-yet clients. It is through this lens of our purpose, our values, and our client experiences that I want to share our analytics—the math that helps us be students of both our results and our potential. Because of our collective efforts to improve our financials, we have been able to invest resources to enhance our products and become a more valued resource for our clients. Your peers just shared two of those situations. We have increased our sales by __ percent, our operating margin by __ percent, and reduced our _____ expenses by __ percent. Let me share a few more details that can help us see how our financial results are impacting us."*

Of the two presentations, which one would better position you to evaluate your organization's performance? Which one positions you to ask better questions?

People quickly learn which metrics ignite the enthusiasm or grumpiness of the organization's leaders. What is not quickly learned are the "Whys." Why the enthusiasm? Why the grumpiness? Why were these metrics chosen over others? Why are the consequences they represent significant?

So given that metrics can be a source of discipline as well as a source of distraction, how do we deliver valued leadership in the area of the organization's math?

I suggest these steps:

1. **Validate**, continually, that the metrics being monitored tie to mission and vision.

2. **Challenge** the "Whys" for selecting these specific metrics.

   • **Q**– *Do they reflect the vitality, risks, and progress of the organization?*

   • **Q**– *Do they hide competitive realities?*

3. **Teach** the "Whys" for selecting these metrics to all stakeholders.

4. **Promote** ownership of the results.

When people know they can impact the metrics, they proudly want to do so. And when all stakeholders understand and own the organization's metrics, a culture of valued leadership thrives.

When associates read wonderfully scripted *"Ain't we something"* statements in the annual report, but seldom hear that same commentary in the context of their daily activities, they lose enthusiasm for the organization. When metrics are mostly what they hear about, metrics are what they assume the organization is about. And when metrics dominate conversations, the employees quickly realize they are one.

Based on my observations, you probably guessed that I did not major in accounting or business analytics in college. I did, however, develop respect for those who did. And I admire those who accept the challenge to help all stakeholders understand the financial math of their organization.

I am not advocating that organizations ignore their metrics. They cannot. I am advocating that metrics be viewed in the context of the organization's purpose for existence. This is what engages associates to generate metrics of success.

Your Professional Beliefs

What are your professional beliefs about how the operational and financial metrics can be shared in your organizations? How are those beliefs impacting your practices? How are those practices impacting the stakeholders? How are they impacting outcomes? Are they surfacing valued leadership?

Chapter 16

Listen and Learn. Then Teach and Coach.

I think organizations create opportunities to positively advance by, first, finding ways to **listen** and **learn**. Then, they continue to positively progress by finding ways to **teach** and **coach**. I think each of us creates opportunities to progress and contribute valued leadership by doing those same things, in that order.

A few years ago I invited several very successful people to participate in a panel discussion. I asked them to share the "Whys" and "Hows" of tactics they were using to:

- Create new client relationships.
- Enhance and retain existing client relationships.
- Increase flows of business.
- Enrich their personal professional lives.

Although their business models and personal styles varied significantly, their practices of listening to and learning from their clients, as well as people who were not yet their clients, were similar. They were all being "students" of these interactions. And because they had first listened and learned, they were prepared to teach and coach. They taught their clients what to expect, how to make sound buying decisions, and how to benefit from the services being offered. They coached their clients to capture the benefits of their services.

Valued leaders are people developers. They grasp the idea that they are the leader of their personal and professional development. They know that, even though self-development is humbling, it is also the permission slip to becoming a valued leader. It is through listening and observing that we discover new opportunities to learn. It is through teaching and coaching that we acquire deeper understanding that enables us to deliver incremental layers of value.

Teaching and coaching is sometimes delivered in the form of a lecture. But it is far more often delivered through conversations, demonstrations, questions, and answers. The most valued content is in the form of perspectives and insights gained through successes and mistakes. The content can take the form of absolutes and mandates, but those are rarely evidence of valued leadership.

Questions Engage Learners in Learning

The easy resource that enables us to listen, learn, teach, and coach is a question. It is amazing what people can teach us when we are genuinely inquisitive (not nosy), ask meaningful (not "'gotcha") questions, and listen to understand (not just to respond). And it is amazing how we can teach and coach when we allow people to be comfortable enough to ask their questions.

We can use **open-ended questions**: *"If you could relive the process of your last project, what components would you insist on retaining for your next project?"* We can ask **closed-ended questions**: *"What percent of our associates training time will be spent in simulations?"* And we can use **probing questions**: *"Our data shows 40 percent of our clients use our xyz service. What are the features and benefits they tell us they value? What factors in their situations could make the features of our abc product attractive to them?"*

Questions can disclose the learner's degree of preparation and comprehension. It is amazing what we can learn by posing challenging questions to ourselves. Here are a few questions for you to ponder:

- **Q–** *What have your clients (as well as the people who have not yet become your clients) been saying to you, asking of you, needing from you?*

- **Q–** *What have you and your organization learned from them?*

- **Q–** *What questions have you been asking of yourself about the next step in your professional development?*

- **Q–** *What **learning-oriented questions** have you been asking that create opportunities to teach and coach?*
    - *During your recent interactions with your clients/ team members/associates about _____, what surprised you? What information or skills would have helped you to teach and coach them?*
    - *What objections and/or concerns did you anticipate hearing that you did not hear? What did you hear that you did not anticipate? How are you modifying your tactics based on these experiences?*

Combining Questions with Coaching

Supportive teaching and coaching can be tied to learning-oriented questions. Here is an example that begins with a lesson learned through a personal experience.

"When I started this career, the details overwhelmed me. I thought I had to memorize all the features of every product. I was nervous. I feared that if I could not answer every possible question or objection the prospect might pose, I would lose the chance to make them a client. Once I realized reference guides and subject matter experts were available to help me, I

was able to move my focus to building my skills to create and enhance client relationships."

Following this teaching message, you ask a question that creates the opportunity to coach. Here is an example: *What would be a significant benefit to your prospect if they take advantage of meeting with you? How will you share that benefit with the prospect?"*

In their book *The War of Art*[4] Steven Pressfield and Shawn Coyne label the enemy that interferes with our lives as "Resistance." I encourage you to get a copy of this book and explore their ideas. Their chapter titled "Unlived Lives" begins with this paragraph, *"Most of us have two lives. The life we live, and the unlived life within us. Between the two stands Resistance."*

What is your resistance to seeing yourself as a valued leader? What is your resistance to finding new ways to contribute valued leadership to your team, your department, your organization?

What are your opportunities to **Listen, Learn, Teach, Coach?**

---

4 *The War of Art: Break Through the Blocks and Win Your Inner Creative Battles*, Steven Pressfield & Shawn Coyne, Copyright 2002, Black Irish Books, ISBN: 978-1-936891-02-3

Chapter 17

Leadership Lessons from Jazz

I enjoy listening to and watching jazz musicians do what they do. Frequently I get to be amazed by the performances of Kansas City jazz musicians. One of them is Kansas City Jazz Walk of Fame saxophonist, educator, and explorer of ideas, Bobby Watson. Bobby is the director of the jazz studies program at the University of Missouri–Kansas City Conservatory of Music and Dance. He is a passionate advocate for the creativity, energy, complexity, and improvisation of jazz. He honors the music through his teaching, performances, and mentoring.

Bobby also honors the music by sharing his insights. Several years ago during a luncheon conversation, Bobby shared his perspectives about the organizational dynamics of a jazz ensemble. He discussed expectations and accountability, research and development, marketing, public relations, entrepreneurial thinking, mission, vision, interpersonal dynamics, and financial metrics.

Even though none of these terms were specifically mentioned, those of us at the luncheon were treated to a wonderfully interesting workshop about organizational dynamics.

Although the reasons for that luncheon were unrelated to this book, Bobby shared relevant observations in response to a question about how a group of jazz musicians become a successful ensemble. His comments were reflective of creating a culture of valued leadership. The setting for Bobby's valued leadership just happened to pertain to the business of the performing arts. It was about enabling each individual in the ensemble to contribute their leadership so the organization, the ensemble, could go places musically they had not yet traveled.

I have heard numerous comments from Bobby that I think are worthy of sharing. With his permission, I share these two:

> *"I am addicted to my imagination."* (Panel discussion during *Convergence of the Arts* exhibition at the American Jazz Museum on April 4, 2014)
>
> *"I don't remember dates of history. I am too busy making history through the music I create."* (UMKC Jazz Friends meeting, July 16, 2014)

As you reflect on these quotes, ask yourself:

> Q- *Am I making history within my sphere of influence?*
>
> Q- *Am I sharing worthy perspectives with my associates, children, and grandchildren?*
>
> Q- *Am I addicted to imagining and creating what could be in my life and in the organizations where I contribute my time and talent?*
>
> Q- *Am I delivering valued leadership?*

I promise you, I am pondering these questions.

And here is one additional question to consider. Are you engaging two key elements of jazz: **listening,** so you can communicate within the ensemble of talent in your organization, and **improvisation,** so you can respond creatively to deliver valued leadership?

The arts have a lot to teach us. Delivering valued leadership to our organizations is a form of art worth developing.

Chapter 18- Valued Leadership
A Final Perspective

Embrace this idea. **You are the leader of the organization called "You. You are the leader of your life.**

The ideas and tactics in this book are wrapped in the context of organizations. Yes, you can use these ideas to deliver valued leadership to your organizations. You can also use these ideas to deliver valued leadership to yourself.

In chapter two I shared the observation that every organization has a culture, planned or not, of assumptions, beliefs, practices, biases, and, of course, some dysfunctional behavior.

Comparably, each of us carries around a set of assumptions, habits, and biases. Each of us is a unique composite of knowledge, skills, competencies, and styles. We engage professional beliefs and practices that are beneficial. We also likely engage professional beliefs and practices that diminish our potential.

Since you are the leader of your professional development, you **"get-to"** define the next steps on that path. You **"get-to"** identify your desired outcomes. You **"get-to"** listen and learn so you can teach and coach.

So I leave you with this question:

"Are you delivering *valued leadership* to the organization called **You**?"

Epilogue

When my first grandson was born, I gave a lot of thought to the idea of being a grandparent. I did not want to just show up for the celebrations; I wanted to contribute value to his life. I wanted him to have fond memories of his time with me. I wanted him to have some "My grandfather always said...did...cared about...challenged me to..." observations that he could share with his pals and his children. In addition to the obvious things like don't run with scissors, don't shoot your eye out with a BB gun, and don't forget the matches when you go on a camping trip, I reflected on what else I wanted to teach him.

I bought a spiral binder to use as a journal to record my memories of events and conversations that my grandson and I would share. On the first few pages of the journal I wrote a list of things I hoped to teach him about life. Here are two items I included:

"Proactiveness beats reactiveness."

"You are the leader of your life."

Each time I write an entry in the journal, I ask myself if I am teaching these lessons.

And I remind myself how lucky I am to have these opportunities.

About The Author

Michael Gerken was born in Kansas City, Missouri in 1946. He began his career in the financial services industry in 1968 after graduating with a business degree from the University of Missouri. He obtained his MBA in Organizational Behavior from the University of Missouri-Kansas City in 1971. He received a Certified Financial Planner Designation in 1979.

A significant portion of Mike's 45-year career focused on the organizational development of his firm and the professional development of the people in that organization. He continues to be engaged in leadership activities in civic and not-for-profit organizations.

Mike enjoys being a student of his life experiences, his children's and grandchildren's commentary, and the fascinating ways that people make things happen.

Bibliography of Leadership Resources

As I referenced in this book, I have studied hundreds of books on leadership. Here are just a few I think you will find useful.

Good to Great, Jim Collins

Mindset: The New Psychology of Success, Carol Dweck, Ph.D.

Drive, Daniel H. Pink

Switch, Chip Heath & Dan Heath

The Effective Executive, Peter Drucker

The Five Most Important Questions, Peter Drucker

Leading at a Higher Level, Ken Blanchard

Leadership BS, by Jeffrey Pfeffer

Leadership Perspectives from History

Books about history provide insights into the complexities of leadership. Leadership is not just about the person. It is also about the context, the situations, where the leadership opportunities occur.

Biographies and stories about historical figures provide insights about leadership. The key is to move past the image or reputations that has been created and find pieces that contributed to that leader's ability to have an impact.

If you enjoy history and discovering insights about people who come to be called leaders, I recommend books such as these:

The Coldest Winter, David Halberstam

Truman, David McCollough

Team of Rivals, Doris Kearns Goodwin

Made in the USA
San Bernardino, CA
23 April 2016